TWO-STITCH
KNITS

TWO-STITCH
KNITS

Jane Crowfoot

Reader's
Digest

Author's Dedication

I would like to dedicate this book to all the Rowan Design Consultants who dedicate their time to teaching and encouraging new and existing knitters. Also to the whole team at Rowan in Holmfirth, England, who make it all possible and give knitters the world over such wonderful yarn to add to their stashes!

A READER'S DIGEST BOOK

This edition published by The Reader's Digest Association, Inc. by arrangement with
Quintet Publishing Limited
6 Blundell Street
London N7 9BH

FOR QUINTET PUBLISHING
Project Editor: Ruth Patrick
Art Direction/Styling: Isobel Gillan, Ruth Patrick
Designers: Isobel Gillan, Rod Teasdale
Photographers: Sian Irvine, Linda Burgess
Models: Daniel Cartwright, Lucy Holliday, Charlotte Holliday, Grace Begley, Laura Begley, Milo Summers, Joanna Arias, Gabriella Stephenson, Kathleen Stephenson, Paola Arias, Lucy Grant, Erica Arias, Gabriel Hall, Magda Arias, Natalie Wu, Jenny Doubt, Chris Lockwood, Kwesi Edman.
Pattern Checker: Penny Hill
Creative Director: Richard Dewing
Publisher: Judith More

FOR READER'S DIGEST
U.S. Project Editor: Marilyn Knowlton
Consulting Editor: Jane Townswick
Canadian Project Editor: Pamela Johnson
Associate Art Director: George McKeon
Cover Design: Mabel Zorzano
Executive Editor, Trade Publishing: Dolores York
President & Publisher, Trade Publishing: Harold Clarke

Library of Congress Cataloging-in-Publication Data
Crowfoot, Jane.
    Two-stitch knits: the quick and easy way to make 50 fast, fun projects /
        Jane Crowfoot. p. cm.
    Includes index.
    ISBN 0-7621-0622-0
    1. Knitting--Patterns.   I. Title.
    TT825.C788 2006
    746.43'2041--dc22

                                                    2005055265

NOTE TO OUR READERS

The editors who produced this book have attempted to make the contents as accurate and correct as possible. Illustrations, photographs, and text have been carefully checked. All instructions should be reviewed and understood by the reader before undertaking any project. The directions and designs for the projects in this publication are under copyright. These projects may be reproduced for the reader's personal use or for gifts. Reproduction for sale or profit is forbidden by law.

Address any comments about *Two-Stitch Knits* to:
The Reader's Digest Association, Inc.
Adult Trade Publishing
Reader's Digest Road
Pleasantville, NY 10570-7000

For more Reader's Digest products and information, visit our web site:
www.rd.com (in the United States)
www.rd.ca (in Canada)
www.readersdigest.com (in Australia)

With special thanks to Early Learning Centre for the loan of toys for photography, and Habitat for the loan of homewares for photography.

Manufactured in Singapore by Pica Digital Pte Ltd. • Printed in China by SNP Leefung Printers Ltd.

1 3 5 7 9 10 8 6 4 2

CONTENTS

Introduction

Knitting is an ancient handicraft, with techniques that have been handed down from generation to generation over the last few millennia. It is extremely difficult to say exactly when and by whom the art of knitting was invented, but there is evidence to suggest that knitted fabrics have been part of civilization for thousands of years.

ABOVE: A *tricoteuse* of the National Convention during the French Revolution. These women were best known for their ghoulish attendance at guillotine executions, circa 1790.

The earliest surviving piece of knitted fabric is a pair of socks with complex color patterning and individual toes, dating back to the time of the ancient Egyptians. Treasures, such as small knitted dolls and keepsakes, have also been found in the tombs of the ancient Mayan tribes.

From documented history, it is clear that whatever the technique, men carried out knitting in these ancient forms, while the task of women was to spin yarn. Europe and the Mediterranean countries seem to have been at the center of the knitting trade. Spanish sailors of the Armada knitted pieces involving many color changes and complex patterns. The small communities or family groups who produced Gansey sweaters from the British Isles would create their own complicated exclusive patterns, which served as a means of identifying sailors' bodies lost at sea.

Early Renaissance paintings depict the Madonna knitting with four needles. Around the sixteenth century, advances in metalworking technology meant that fine-gauge knitting needles were becoming easier to produce. Knitting became a thriving trade, with men training for up to six years to become a Master Guild knitter, producing stockings, gloves, and wall hangings containing intricate flora and fauna designs.

Elizabeth I of England had a passion for silk stockings with lace patterns knitted to an incredibly fine gauge. During her reign, a more primitive style of knitting was commonly produced by small farming communities that used it as a way to supplement their income, with each member of a family producing and selling a pair of stockings weekly. By the seventeenth century, hand knitting was a trade usually practiced only by the lower classes.

As people began to travel the globe, the practice of knitting became more widespread, and by the nineteenth century, hand knitting had become a leisure activity among the middle classes, with women producing mufflers and fine, beaded purses. The quality of yarns improved greatly, and fine cotton became available for knitters interested in making intricate shawls and petticoats.

During the Second World War, many people contributed to the war effort by knitting socks and gloves for servicemen. With yarns on ration, the saying "make do and mend" was born, and many knitters unraveled old sweaters in order to reknit another type of garment.

Although nylon was produced by Dupont in 1938, synthetic yarns were not widely available until after the war. By the 1950s, the look and feel of knitting yarn had changed quite dramatically. Most synthetic fibers, which are derived from coal or petroleum, became a cheaper alternative to wool or cotton fibers. With advances in technology, blended knitting yarns were produced, and yarns containing mohair, alpaca, and even cashmere became more readily available to the public.

Around this time, haute couture also played a major role in the growth of the hand-knitting industry. Hand-knitted ski jumpers and fitted women's cardigans were fashionable, and *Vogue* produced hundreds of elegant knitting patterns. Housewives had much more time on their hands, because washing machines replaced scrubbing boards and mangles, while gas and electric ovens replaced the open ranges. Women found time to enjoy knitting and sewing.

Over the past 50 years, advances in technology and industry have made machine-knitted fabrics accessible and inexpensive, which means that hand knitting is no longer viewed as a necessity. The current upsurge in the popularity of hand knitting has more to do with lifestyle choices; knitting is seen as a fun and therapeutic hobby with gratifying end results. Knitting is currently at the forefront of popular crafts and leisure-time activities, and has been referred to as "the new yoga." Many celebrities, models, and actresses are forming an addictive knitting habit, thereby publicizing the craft and thrusting it to the forefront of the media.

Many new knitters strive to stretch the boundaries of their creativity to produce personalized knitted fabrics and garments. Knitters today want to produce items to cherish, projects that bear the stamp of originality and the time that has gone into their production, while displaying a professional polish.

The demise of the extended family in Western culture may mean that knitters no longer have access to a relative or friend for guidance, so as a result, knitting clubs and groups are popping up all over the country. People are coming together to "stitch and bitch" or just to

ABOVE: Usherettes at a cinema knitting socks for servicemen during the Second World War.

ABOVE: Marilyn Monroe knitting in George Cukor's 1960 film *Let's Make Love,* giving the craft valuable publicity.

"knit and chat." Groups meet at one another's houses, bookstores, coffee bars, and university classrooms. Rowan Yarns now run hundreds of knitting workshops and provide yarn stores with design consultants to help young shoppers choose yarns and patterns.

A knitted fabric is made up of just two stitches—a plain stitch and a purl stitch. Once these are mastered, no pattern is impossible to knit! These two stitches can create the simplest of knitted fabrics, such as garter or stockinette stitch; when used in more complicated sequences, they can create intricate lace patterns and textures. The ways in which these two stitches can combine to produce a knitted fabric are unlimited.

Two-Stitch Knits is the perfect companion for a beginner knitter and anyone wishing to rekindle their knitting passion. It features fully illustrated technique instructions, showing you how to start from scratch, with stylish color photography and expertly designed patterns for simple yet beautiful knitted pieces that you will love to own or enjoy giving as unique gifts to family and friends.

The simple step-by-step instructions will ease you into the knitter's world, starting with the basics, such as holding the needles and casting on, and working a plain stitch and a purl to produce a knitted fabric. As your confidence increases, you may want to explore the fun in color knitting, beading, or simple lace stitching. *Two-Stitch Knits* will show you how, once you have mastered the basics, you can go on to create the 50 gorgeous projects in this book, including textured cushions, colorful hats, scarves, afghans, bags, and simple garments worked in sumptuous Rowan yarns.

Equipment and Helpful Hints

All you need to create a knitted fabric is a pair of knitting needles and some yarn. However, other pieces of equipment will come in handy as your skills increase.

Knitting Needles

Knitting needles come in various lengths and circumferences. In most cases, the size will be marked either on the side of the needle or on the "stopper" at the end. The size of the needles required for any project is determined by the thickness of the yarn and the number of stitches the project requires.

Large plastic or wooden needles are often used for knitting chunky yarns (see page 18). Small plastic needles are usually used by children or beginners, since the needles are light and easy to hold (see page 34). Bamboo needles are especially good for knitting with cotton, as they are slightly more slippery than plastic or aluminium (see below). Aluminum needles are probably the most common type because they are inexpensive and readily available.

Circular knitting needles are two short needles joined together by a filament of plastic or metal (see below). These allow you to knit "in the round" to produce tubular knitting (such as socks). When working in the round, you need to work only *knit* or *plain* rows (see page 24) because your work does not need to be turned at the end of each row. However, circular needles can also be used in the same way as a pair of traditional needles by working knit and purl rows and turning the work at the end of each row.

Traditionally, knitting needles were made from wood or bone, but today's most popular needles are more likely to be made from plastic, aluminum, or bamboo.

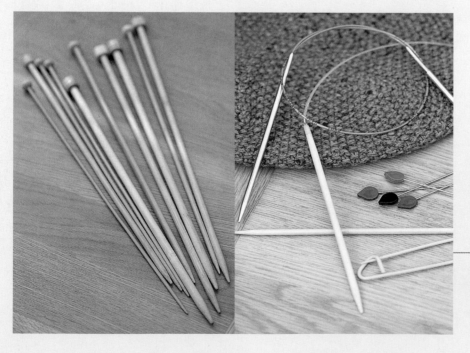

Needle Gauge and Ruler

A needle gauge with a ruler is handy if you own knitting needles without size markings. Simply slide a needle through successive holes until you find the size of the needle. The printing by the side of the hole that fits your needle tells you the needle size. One side has a ruler, while the other side shows the needle gauge (see page 11).

LEFT (Clockwise from top): Metal and bamboo circular needles, knitter's pins, and stitch holder.

FAR LEFT: Bamboo needles in various sizes.

Row Counters

These come in different sizes, depending on the knitting needle thickness, and are used to help you count the number of rows you have worked. They are particularly useful when working complicated lace or cable patterns. The outer plastic cover houses a small dial with numbers printed on it (see page 24). At the end of each row, you can simply turn the dial to the next number.

Scissors and Tape Measure

A pair of small sharp scissors is an essential tool for trimming loose yarn ends (see page 12). As you make a knitted project, you will often be required to take measurements. It is a good idea to have a tape measure that has inches and centimeters clearly marked on the same side (see right).

Safety Pins and Stitch Holders

You will find these particularly useful when working on a larger project, such as a sweater or a cardigan, where stitches need to be left unworked in order to add a neckline later on. Stitches can unravel easily when slipped off a knitting needle so a safety pin or stitch holder is helpful for saving the stitches from dropping (see page 10). Stitch holders come in various sizes, depending on the number of stitches that need to be held. The stitches slip from the knitting needle onto the holder in the same way as you would slip a stitch from one needle to another (see Slipping a Knit Stitch, page 30 *and* Slipping a Purl Stitch, page 31).

Point Protectors

These protect the points of your knitting needles and prevent your knitting from slipping off the needles when you are not working on your project (see above). They are especially handy if you carry your knitting around with you in a knitting bag or basket, and they help you avoid being stabbed by the unprotected needle points.

Pins and Needles

Choose pins with brightly colored tips, as they are much easier to see. The most common pins found in stores are the plastic-headed straight pins most commonly used for dressmaking—these are fine if you need to pin only a small area (see above). It is also possible to buy specific knitter's pins that are longer and thicker and have large, flat heads—these tend to be a little more stable than dressmaking pins (see page 10).

Knitter's sewing, or tapestry, needles come in various sizes. The eye needs to be large enough to accommodate the knitting yarn, and the point should be relatively blunt (see page 12).

ABOVE (Clockwise from left): Needle gauge and ruler, straight pins, tape measure, and point protectors.

Stitch Markers

Stitch markers are used as an alternative to knitter's pins and are extremely handy for counting stitches and pattern repeats (see page 44). They can be slipped through a knitted stitch and caught onto the yarn, or they can be placed over the knitting needle when beginning a large cast-on.

Yarn Bobbins

When using different colors in a Fair Isle or Intarsia designs you may find it easier to wind small amounts of yarn around a bobbin instead of working directly from the ball (see left). The yarn is wrapped around the bobbin and sits between the spokes at either end, much like the string holders on a kite.

ABOVE (Clockwise from top right): Scissors, yarn bobbins, needles, needle holder, and stitch holder.

Yarns and Ply

Most fibers need to be processed in some way to form yarn. Each strand of fiber is known as a ply. A yarn is made up of a number of plys spun together in different ways to create differing thicknesses of yarn.

Choosing yarn is the most important decision any knitter has to make, since the finished appearance of any project can depend completely on the quality of the yarn. It is really important to choose not only the correct color and ply of yarn but also to consider a fiber's suitability to a project.

Yarns are made up of a number of plys spun together. Yarns tend to be referred to in specific weights, i.e. 4-ply (traditionally made from 4 yarns twisted together). This is not always the case, however, as yarns are also produced singly to knit to a certain gauge. The general rule is that the lower the ply, the finer the yarn.

Yarn content falls into three main categories: those of animal origin, such as wool, cashmere, and angora; those of plant origin, such as cotton and linen; and those of synthetic or man-made, such as rayon and polyamid yarns.

Substituting Yarns

There are some fabulous yarns to choose from these days, so don't fall into the trap of thinking that you have to use the exact yarn or color specified in a pattern.

When substituting yarn, it is important that you stick to the same number of plys per strand. For example, if a pattern is written for a 4-ply yarn with a high wool content, you could decide to substitute a 4-ply cotton. However you could not substitute a 4-ply yarn for a Sport-weight yarn, because it is much thicker.

If you do decide to use a substitute yarn, consider the meterage of each ball. For example, if the pattern requires 10 balls of wool and each ball contains 120 meters of yarn, then the total meterage used in the project is 1,200 meters. If the substitute yarn has only 80 meters per ball, you will need more than 10 balls. To calculate how many more, divide the total meterage (1,200) by the substitute meterage (80): $200 \div 80 = 15$. (If in doubt, always buy a little extra.)

Ball-Band Information

Most yarns have a ball band or tag of some sort that gives you important information. The heading on the band shows the company logo, the specific name of the yarn, and the yarn weight—in this case, the yarn is *handknit cotton*.

The band will also tell you what the yarn is made from, i.e. cotton, wool etc. The weight and the approximate length of the yarn will also be shown. Most yarns sold commercially come in certain weights, usually 50 g or 100 g, although it is possible to purchase yarn in larger amounts, especially when using acrylic yarns, which are sometimes sold in 200 g balls.

There may be symbols or written instructions on washing and drying guidelines, and the shade and dye-lot number on the ball band. It is important that all of the yarn for a project comes from the same dye lot. Slight differences in color may not be immediately apparent in certain light, but could be horribly obvious in a knitted piece.

The most important piece of information is the graph that shows the knitting gauge and the guide to needle sizes. In this case, the yarn should knit to a gauge of 19/20 stitches and 28 rows to 4 in. / 10 cm on size 6 (4 mm) needles (see Gauge and Tension pages 15 *and* 35).

BELOW: Rowan yarns are available in a multitude of colors and textures.

Washing and Care Essentials

When knitted in a quality yarn and cared for in the correct manner, a hand-knit garment can last for many years. Keep the ball band so you can refer to it when you need to launder the knitted fabric. Before making any decisions about how to care for an item, always check the ball band for as much information as possible.

Before immersing the item in water, remove any non-washable trims, such as buttons or braid. Avoid using biological washing powders or those with any kind of added brighteners. Soap flakes, mild detergent, and specially formulated liquids are usually best.

Make sure the water is cool and the detergent is completely dissolved. If the detergent needs warm or hot water in order to disperse thoroughly, make sure it has had time to cool before you begin. Wash one garment at a time and change the water after every piece. Do not wring, twist, or rub the fabric, and never use a brush to remove spots or stains. Wash the garment as quickly as possible, although some pieces can be left to soak for short lengths of time. Make sure the water runs clear after the final rinse.

If you are machine washing a knitted project, use a delicate or wool cold-water cycle with minimal fast spin action. It is preferable to put delicate garments in a net bag or tied pillowcase before spinning.

Drying and blocking

Blocking is the term used to describe the laying out of the knitted piece prior to sewing it together, or to reshape a finished piece once it has been washed.

Lay the garment or knitted piece flat on a clean dry towel or raised sweater dryer. It may be necessary to pin the item if it is prone to curling or if it needs to be slightly stretched. Pieces to be joined together should be blocked with the right side facing down and secured with straight knitter's pins. Leave to dry away from direct sunlight or a heat source. Careful blocking of a damp garment should eliminate the need to steam or press it after it is dry.

Steaming and Pressing

Knitted fabrics and irons are not a good combination. It is very easy to scorch a knitted fabric or overpress it. Once the damage has been done, it is often irreversible.

If you do need to steam or press a piece of knitted fabric, pin it out as described for blocking. Place a damp cloth over the fabric and press very gently with a warm, dry iron.

For cabled or textured pieces, hold a steam iron over the top of the cloth and allow the steam to pass through to the knitted fabric. Do not put any pressure on the iron, because this will flatten stitch detailing.

How to Read a Pattern

BELOW: Carefully selecting buttons, beads, and other embellishments can add a professional finish to your garment.

There is certain information contained in every written pattern regardless of the company that has produced it, and it is very important that you read through the entire pattern before starting to knit any project.

Patterns are often written for more than one size and will give these in either age, dress size, or chest/bust measurement. In this book, the smallest size is shown first, with subsequent sizes shown in parentheses. This principle also applies for yarn quantities, numbers of stitches, and any other measurements. There should also be at least three finished measurements given. These are the chest/bust measurement taken under arm, the length from the shoulder to the bottom edge, and the sleeve length from the beginning of the cuff to the widest point of the sleeve top. In some cases there may be a schematic drawing showing these measurements and the general shape of the garment. To avoid any mistakes when following a pattern with more than one size, it is a good idea to circle all figures for the size you wish to make before you commence.

Yarn amounts, needle sizes, and any extra equipment and materials will also appear at the beginning of a pattern.

Abbreviations

The patterns in this book feature a number of standard abbreviations, which are explained below. These abbreviations are logical and easy to understand.

alt	alternate	rem	remain
cm	centimeters	rep	repeat
cont	continue	rs	right side
dec	decrease	skpo	slip one stitch, knit one stitch, pass
foll	following		slipped stitch over
g st	garter st	sl	slip
in	inch(es)	st	stitch
inc	increase	st st	stockinette stitch
k	knit	tbl	through back of loop
m1	make 1 stitch	tog	together
m1pw	make 1 stitch purlwise	ws	wrong side
p	purl	yf	yarn forward to make a stitch
patt	pattern	yrn	yarn around needle to make a stitch

TIP: When choosing which size garment to knit, measure an existing garment that fits you really well and compare it to the measurements given in the pattern. By choosing the size that has the closest measurements to an existing garment, you can be sure of getting the right fit.

It is very important to knit a gauge swatch before beginning a project to ensure that it turns out the correct size and shape. The pattern will list the number of stitches and rows to 4 in. (10 cm). If you find you have more stitches and rows to 4 in. (10 cm), use a larger knitting needle. If you have worked fewer stitches and rows, use a larger needle to achieve the correct gauge (see Gauge and Tension, page 35). The diameter of the knitting needle affects the size of the stitch, so stitches knitted on a chunky needle will take up more space than those knitted on a fine needle. Be aware that your own gauge can change with practice, but it can also be dependent on your mood or the situation in which you are knitting.

Gauge Swatches

The tension is correct; therefore the sample piece is the correct size.

The tension is too loose; therefore the sample piece is larger.

The tension is too tight; therefore the sample piece is smaller.

Techniques *getting started*

Holding the Needles

A knitted fabric is created by working combinations of only two different stitches on a pair of knitting needles after a cast-on row. The way that the needles are held can vary, but the three most common positions are as follows:

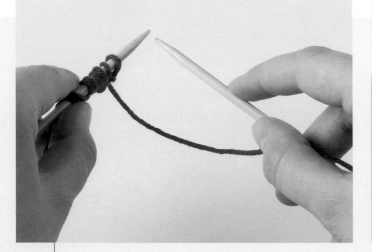

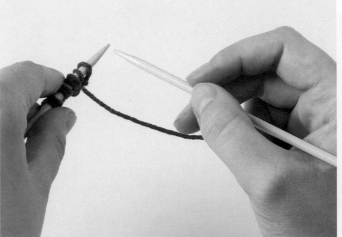

Scottish or English Method:

Both needles are held from above. The left hand takes the weight of the needles while the stitch is being made. The yarn is held in the right hand.

French Method:

The left needle is held from above as for the Scottish method, but the right needle is held from underneath as if holding a pencil. The knitting needle rests in the gap between your thumb and index finger and the yarn is held in the right hand.

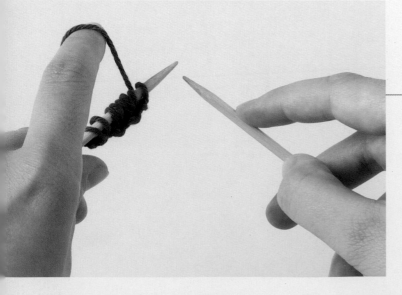

Continental or German Method:

This is considered a speedy way to knit! The needles are held as for the Scottish method, but the yarn is held in the left hand.

Making a Slip Knot

A knitted fabric is made by working rows of stitches in various sequences. In order to create a fabric, you must first make a base row known as a cast-on row. A slip knot is used as the first stitch for a cast-on row and is made as follows:

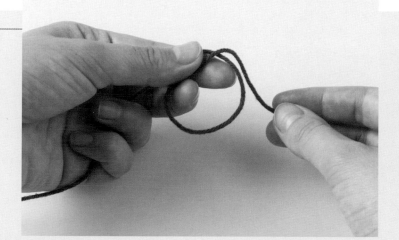

1 Holding the yarn in both hands, make a small loop in the yarn. Take the piece that you are holding in the right hand underneath the loop.

2 Pull this piece of yarn through the original loop, so that it pulls through to create a knot. Do not pull the short end of the yarn through the loop.

3 Place the slip knot onto the knitting needle.

Casting On

Once you have created the initial slip knot, you are ready to cast on. There are many different ways to cast on, each giving a slightly different appearance. A good cast-on allows you to work the first row with ease and should be neat and even. There are two methods of casting on that are most commonly used; they are the Thumb Method and the Cable Cast On.

The Thumb Method

This method uses only one knitting needle, so it is very quick and creates a stretchy edge that is good for hats, bags, and children's garments. The slip knot that forms the first stitch must be far enough along the yarn to create two ends. The yarn on one side of the knot will lead to the ball, and the yarn on the other will be a tail end. It is important that the tail end is long enough to create the number of stitches needed for the cast-on.

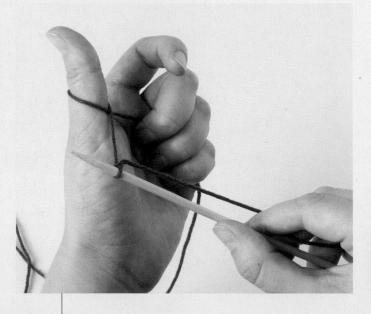

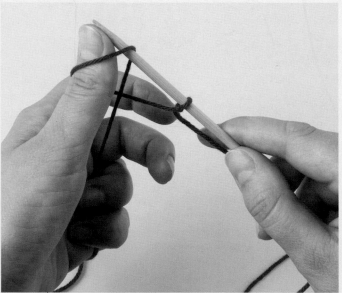

1 Place the slip knot on the knitting needle and hold it in your right hand. *Hold the tail end of yarn under the little finger of your left hand and wrap it around your thumb from front to back, holding the ball end of yarn in your right hand.

2 Slide the knitting needle through the loop on your thumb, as shown.

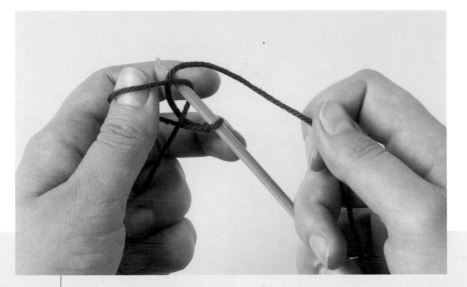

3 Wrap the yarn held in your
right hand around the knitting
needle counterclockwise from
back to front.

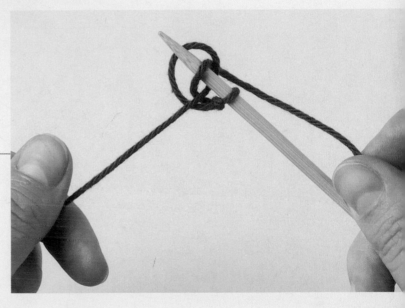

4 Transfer the loop from your
thumb onto the knitting needle.

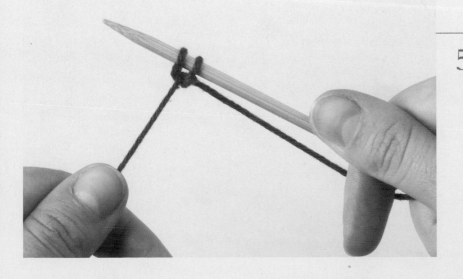

5 Pull the yarn held in the left hand to tighten
the stitch and repeat from * in Step 1 until
you have cast on the required number
of stitches.

The Cable Method

This cast-on method uses both knitting needles and creates a strong edge with a double thickness of yarn. You do not need to allow for a tail end of yarn, as in the thumb method. The ball end of yarn is held in the right hand, but the tail end of yarn is not used and therefore can be short.

1 Place the slip knot on the knitting needle and hold the needle in your left hand. Slide the right knitting needle through the loop created by the slip knot from front to back.

2 Using the right hand, wrap the yarn around the right knitting needle counterclockwise from back to front.

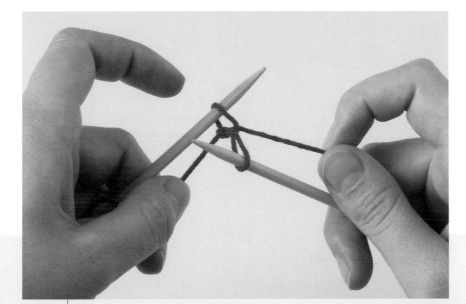

3 Slide the right needle through the loop
  on the left needle, catching the wrapped
  yarn and bringing it through the loop to
  create another loop.

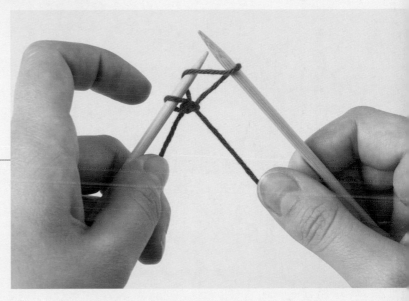

4 Pass the left needle over the top of the new loop,
  placing the tip of the needle through the loop on
  the right needle. Remove the right needle, thus
  transferring the stitch to the left.

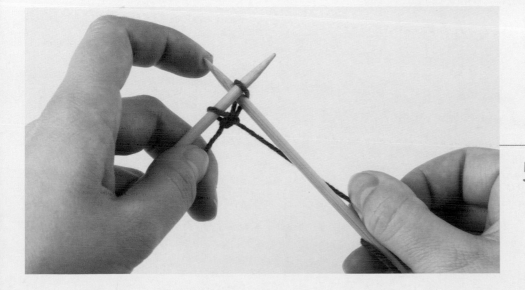

5 Make each subsequent stitch
  by placing the right needle
  between the last two stitches
  made on the left needle, and
  repeating Steps 2 through 4.

Producing a Knitted Fabric

Once you have completed a satisfactory cast-on edge, you will be ready to start producing a knitted fabric.

Knitting a Stitch

The first and most basic stitch to learn is the *knit* (or *plain*) stitch.

1 Cast on the required number of stitches and hold the needle with these stitches in your left hand. Hold the yarn at the back of the work and slide the right needle through the stitch on the left needle from front to back.

2 Using the right hand, wrap the yarn around the right knitting needle counterclockwise from back to front.

3 Slide the right needle through the stitch on the left needle, catching the wrapped yarn and bringing it through the stitch to create a loop on the right needle. Slide the yarn from the left needle and let it drop. Repeat Steps 1 through 3 for each stitch on the left needle.

Purling a Stitch

A *purl* stitch creates a more textured stitch than a knit stitch. It is commonly used on the reverse of the work, but it can be used to create interesting textural stitch combinations.

1 Holding the knitting in your left hand and the yarn at the front of the work, slide the right needle through the stitch on the left needle from right to left.

2 Using the right hand, wrap the yarn around the right knitting needle counterclockwise.

3 Slide the right needle back through the stitch on the left needle, catching the wrapped yarn and bringing it through the stitch to create a loop on the right needle. Slide the yarn from the left needle and let it drop.

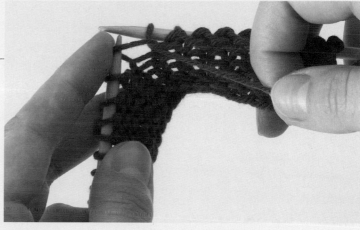

Turning the Work

At the end of every row, you must turn the work in order to begin the next row. As you complete a row of stitches, the left needle becomes empty and the stitches are transferred to the right needle. Once all stitches have been worked, swap the empty needle held in the right hand to the left hand and begin the next row.

Basic Stitch Variations

All knitting, however complicated, is made up of combinations of just two stitches: the knit and the purl stitches.

Garter Stitch

If you were to work rows of just knit, or rows of just purl stitches in succession, you would create a knitted fabric known as *garter stitch*. This is quite textural and sturdy and looks the same on both sides of the fabric.

Stockinette Stitch

This fabric is different on both sides and therefore has a *right side*, or *front*, and a *wrong side*, or *back*. The sides of the fabric are also respectively referred to as a *knit side* and a *purl side*.

The right side is smooth, and you will be able to see that the stitches create a zig-zag effect. The wrong side is bumpy and looks a little like the garter stitch.

To make a fabric using the stockinette stitch, work alternate rows of knit stitches and rows of purl stitches. If you have the smooth side of the fabric facing you as you begin the row, you will need to work a knit row in order to keep the pattern correct. If you have the more textural side facing you at the beginning of the row, you will need to work a purl row.

Working knit and purl stitches in the same row

If you want to create textural relief patterns, you will need to work both knit and purl stitches in the same row. It is important that you change from a knit to a purl stitch and visa versa in the correct way.

Changing from a knit stitch to a purl stitch

1 Having completed a knit stitch, the yarn will be held at the reverse of the work.

2 In order to work a subsequent purl stitch, bring the yarn through to the front of the work between both knitting needles. Then purl the next stitch.

Changing from a purl stitch to a knit stitch

1 Having completed a purl stitch, the yarn will be held at the front of the work.

2 In order to work a subsequent knit stitch, take the yarn to the back of the work between both knitting needles. Then knit the next stitch.

Working Stitches Together

You may be required to work two or more stitches together in techniques such as lacework and when shaping a knitted piece. This will be done either as an instruction to knit stitches together or purl them together.

Knitting Two Stitches Together

1 Slide the right needle through the first two stitches on the left needle from front to back.

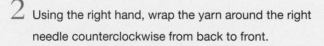

2 Using the right hand, wrap the yarn around the right needle counterclockwise from back to front.

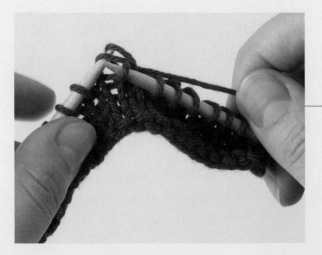

3 Slide the right needle through both stitches on the left needle, catching the wrapped yarn and bringing it through the stitches to create a loop on the right needle. Slide the stitches from the left needle and let them drop so that the new stitch transfers to the right needle.

Purling Two Stitches Together

1 Slide the right needle through the first two stitches on the left needle from right to left.

2 Using the right hand, wrap the yarn around the right needle counterclockwise.

3 Slide the right needle back through the stitches on the left needle, catching the wrapped yarn and bringing it through the stitches to create a loop on the right needle. Slide the stitches from the left needle and let them drop so that the new stitch transfers to the right needle.

Slipping a Stitch

In order to create some textural fabrics such as lace, or when shaping a piece of knitting, you may be required to slip stitches.

Slipping a Knit Stitch (also known as Slipping a Stitch *Knitwise*)

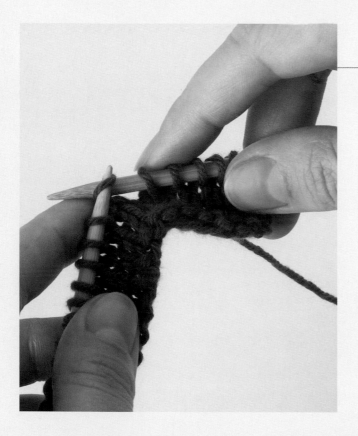

1   Slide the right knitting needle through the stitch on the left needle from front to back, as if to knit.

2   Let the stitch drop from the left knitting needle and pass onto the right needle.

Slipping a Purl Stitch (also known as Slipping a Stitch *Purlwise*)

1 Slide the right knitting needle through the stitch on the left needle from right to left as if to purl.

2 Let the stitch drop from the left knitting needle and pass onto the right needle.

Making a Stitch

There will be times when you will need to increase the number of stitches in a row. This may be when you are shaping a garment or when you need more stitches to accommodate a stitch pattern, such as for lace patterns. There are a few ways of doing this, but the most reliable one is as follows:

1 Pass the right knitting needle underneath the "bar" of yarn between two stitches from front to back.

2 Slip the yarn to the left needle and remove the right needle.

3 Slide the right needle behind the yarn on the left needle from right to left. (This is called "knitting through the back loop.")

4 Knit the new stitch by wrapping the yarn around the right needle counterclockwise.

5 Slide the right needle through the new stitch on the left needle, catching the yarn in as you do so. Remove the left needle, passing the new stitch onto the right needle.

Binding Off

Once you have completed the section you are working on, you will need to bind off the stitches in order to prevent them from unraveling.

1 Knit two stitches onto the right needle.

2 Slide the left needle through the first stitch on the right needle from left to right.

3 Bring this stitch over the top of the second stitch on the right needle and drop from the left needle. Knit another stitch and repeat from Step 2 until all stitches have been worked from the needles. When you reach the final stitch, cut the yarn and slip the stitch from the needle, being careful not to unravel your work. Pass the cut end of yarn through the loop created by the final stitch and pull to tighten and secure.

Gauge or Tension

It is very important that your knitted project is worked to the correct gauge. This means that the number of stitches measured over a specified distance (usually 4 in. / 10 cm) match those instructed on the ball band or by the pattern. If you have knitted either too tightly or too loosely, then your finished project will be the wrong size. Not only that, but the amount of yarn that you require to complete the project will change. It is important that you work a gauge swatch before you embark on any project.

Measuring and Counting Gauge

1 Lay your knitted gauge swatch flat. Using a flat ruler (*not* a tape measure), measure across a horizontal row of stitches and place a marker pin at the 4 in. / 10 cm point. Do the same for the vertical rows of stitches.

The sample shown at right has a garter-stitch selvage. This is done by knitting the first and last stitches of each purl row. The selvage edges can prevent the fabric from curling, and they make useful guides when sewing a project together.

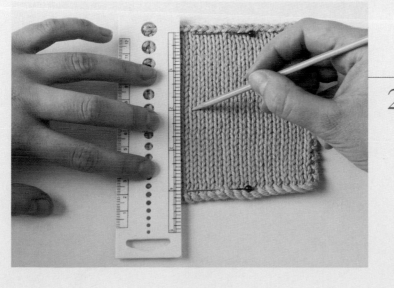

2 Use the point of a knitting needle to count the number of stitches and rows between each pin.

Sewing Knitted Fabrics Together

When you have spent a lot of time working on a knitted project, it is important to sew it together as neatly as possible. There are many different stitches that can be used, but the simplest and neatest is the mattress stitch.

Mattress Stitch

This stitch is worked on the right side of the knitted fabric and can be used on all stitches, not just the stockinette stitch (as shown). The sample shown uses a different color in order to clearly show the formation of the sewn stitches—however, it is advisable to sew up in the same color yarn as your knitting so the join is not visible. It is a good idea to start sewing up after a welt (i.e. the cuff on a cardigan). In this case, we have worked in stockinette stitch, so we have counted up a few rows. When the edge is completely sewn together, turn the work and use the tail end of the yarn to sew up to the bottom edge with mattress stitch. It is a good idea to work on a flat surface.

1   Thread a tapestry needle with a length of cut yarn. Working on the left-hand piece of knitting, insert the needle through the knitted piece one stitch in from the edge of the work. The appearance of this stitch will differ depending on what pattern you have worked the fabric in (i.e. stockinette stitch, garter stitch, etc.). The best way to identify the first stitch is to make sure that you have put the needle through the work *after* the yarns that form both sides of the stitch. If need be, count the stitches in order to identify the first stitch. Once the needle is inserted through the work, count two "bars" of yarn and bring the needle through to the front again, as shown at left. The bars are there, whatever stitch you have worked in. The bar is the yarn that sits in the space between stitches (see Making a Stitch, page 32).

2 Take the needle across to the right-hand fabric and insert the needle through the knitted piece one stitch in from the edge of the work. Count two "bars" of yarn and bring the needle through to the front, as shown above.

3 On the left-hand fabric, insert the needle through the same hole through which the yarn from the previous stitch protrudes. Count two "bars" of yarn and bring the needle through to the front again, as shown above.

4 Bring the needle through the bars and repeat Step 3 on the right side.

5 You can leave the stitches loose for a couple of inches. Then tighten them, by holding the knitted pieces flat and pulling the sewing yarn until the pieces are drawn together.

Troubleshooting

Once you have mastered the basics of knitting, it is really important that you take the time to understand how yarn creates the stitch formation; in other words, what a stitch looks like and how it is joined to the stitch either side of it and those above and below. Once you can do this, you will find it much easier not only to count rows and stitches, but also to recognize and correct mistakes.

Check your work for mistakes frequently, say every couple of rows, because the more knitting you do after making the mistake, the more time-consuming it will be to correct it. It may be a good idea to work a sample piece of knitting on which to practice the following techniques.

Picking Up a Dropped Stitch

If you have accidentally dropped a stitch from your knitting needle, don't panic!

1 If a stitch is allowed to drop, it will unravel.

2 Place the right needle through the center of the dropped stitch from front to back.

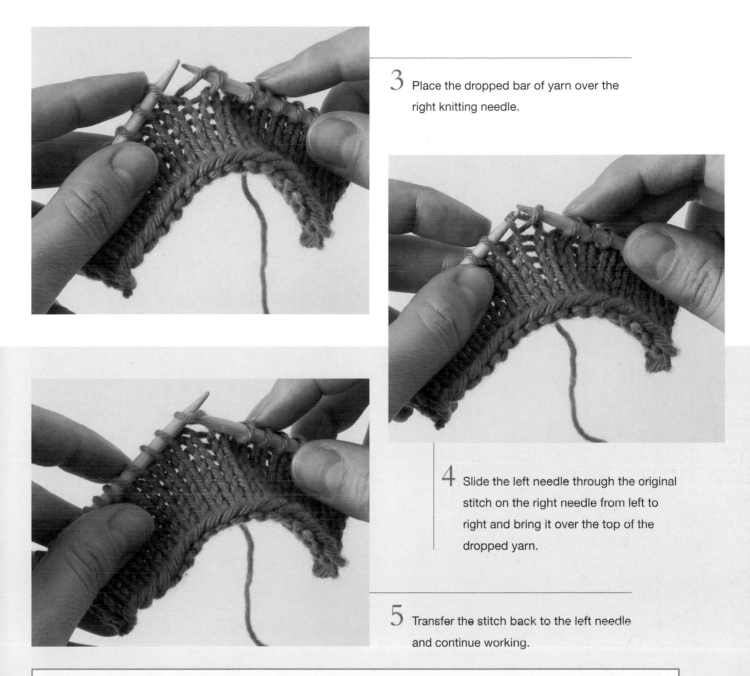

3 Place the dropped bar of yarn over the right knitting needle.

4 Slide the left needle through the original stitch on the right needle from left to right and bring it over the top of the dropped yarn.

5 Transfer the stitch back to the left needle and continue working.

In garter stitch, or if you need to reproduce a purl stitch on the right side of your work, you will need to rework the stitch differently after you have picked it up.

To do this, follow Steps 1 and 2, making sure that the bar of yarn (the dropped yarn) sits at the *front* of the work.

Transfer the stitch from the right needle to the left.

Put the right needle through the stitch on the left needle from right to left as if to purl the stitch.

Catch the dropped yarn by placing the right needle underneath it from top to bottom.

Push the bar back through the stitch with the right needle.

Unpicking Stitches

If you have made a mistake earlier on in a row, you will need to unpick the stitches in that row in order to rectify it. It is important that you do not twist the stitches, because this will affect the appearance of your knitting.

Unpicking Stitches on a Knit Row

1 Pinpoint the mistake. In this case, it is a purl stitch worked in a knit row.

2 Place the left needle through the center of the stitch *below* the first stitch on the right knitting needle.

3 Pass the stitch from the right knitting needle to the left needle and pull the yarn to unravel the stitch above it. Repeat until you reach the mistake. Rework the "mistake" stitch and continue knitting as before.

Unpicking Stitches on a Purl Row

1 Pinpoint the mistake. In this case, it is a knit stitch worked in a purl row.

2 Place the left needle through the center of the stitch *below* the first stitch on the right needle.

3 Pass the stitch from the right knitting needle to the left needle and pull the yarn to unravel the stitch above it. Repeat until you reach the mistake. Rework the "mistake" stitch and continue knitting as before.

Joining in a New Yarn

When you near the end of a ball of yarn, you will need to join in a new one. This should not be done mid-row, because this can cause a hole that will be obvious from the front of your work.

1 Slide the right needle into the first stitch on the left needle, from front to back.

2 Lay the new yarn over both needles with the tail end of yarn to the back of the work.

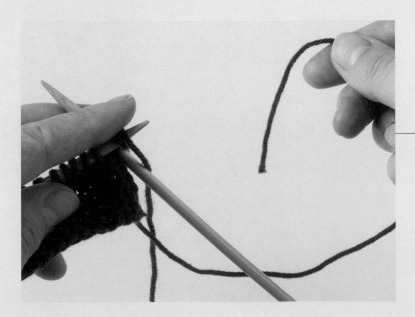

3 Cross the finished end over the top of the new yarn and drop (also see Step 2, page 49).

4 Pick up the new end of yarn, holding the finished end securely in your right hand.

5 Using the new end of yarn, knit the stitch by taking it around the right needle counterclockwise.

6 Slide the right needle through the stitch on the left needle and under the tail end of yarn. Remove the left needle and allow the stitch to transfer to the right needle.

This technique is the same, whether you are working a knit or purl stitch; simply work whichever stitch is applicable. When adding a new yarn, it is always best to do it either at the beginning or end of a knit row, depending upon how much yarn you have.

Unraveling Stitches

It is important that you check your work for mistakes at frequent intervals. If you find that you have made a mistake a little way down the work, you will need to unravel it. The process is the same, whatever type of stitch pattern you are working.

1 Pinpoint the mistake. In this case, it is a purl stitch that has been worked on a right-side row of stockinette stitch.

2 Carefully remove your knitting needle, hold your work flat, and gently pull the yarn to unravel the stitches up to the row beyond the "mistake" stitch. The yarn should be at the left side of your work.

3 Slide the right knitting needle through the center of every stitch from right to left. It is important that you slip the stitches back on the needle correctly. To do this, make sure that the yarn that forms the right-hand side of the stitch loop sits at the front of your knitting needle. Continue knitting.

Beading

This is a decorative technique for positioning beads within your knitted fabric. The beads are threaded onto the knitting yarn before you cast on, and can be placed randomly or in a pattern sequence, depending on the design featured in your project. The beads "sit" on the yarn and can be pushed out of the way when not in use. If you run out of beads, simply cut the knitting yarn and add in more.

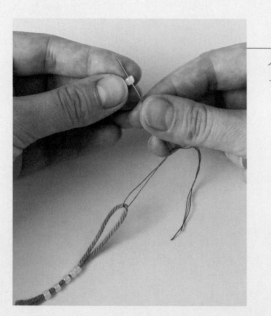

1 To thread beads onto the knitting yarn, you will need to create a loop in a piece of sewing thread, through which the knitting yarn is subsequently threaded. To do this, you can either thread a sewing needle with cotton thread and put a small knot in it to create a loop, or you can thread both ends of the sewing cotton through the sewing needle, thus also creating a loop. Put the knitting yarn through the loop created by the sewing cotton. Thread the beads down over the needle, onto the cotton sewing thread, and then down onto the knitting yarn.

2 Cast on and knit stitches as required for your project. All beads are placed in the same way; in the example shown here, some beads have already been placed on previous rows. Work to where the next bead is to be placed. Slide a bead up to the top of the knitting yarn until it can't go any further.

3 Bring the yarn forward between both knitting needles.

4 Slip the next stitch on the left needle purl wise (see Slipping a Purl Stitch, page 31).

5 Making sure that the bead sits in front of the slipped stitch, take the yarn back between the two knitting needles and knit the following stitch.

Color Work

As your knitting skills improve you may decide that you wish to tackle some color work. There are two main color techniques: Intarsia and Fair Isle. The Rainbow Toy Bag (see page 86), the Tote Bag (see page 102), and the Summer Garden Cushion (see page 154) feature Intarsia knitting, and the Pastel Beaded Cardigan (see page 107) features Fair Isle.

Joining in a New Color

Whichever type of color work you are doing, you will need to learn how to join in a new color of yarn. This can be done either at the beginning, end, or midway through a row.

1 Slide the right knitting needle into the stitch on the left needle from front to back. Lay the new yarn over both needles with the tail end of yarn at the back of the work.

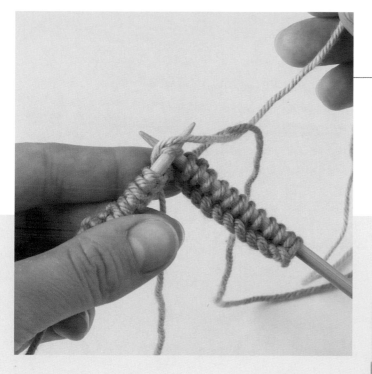

2 Cross the finished yarn over the top of the new yarn and drop.

3 Using the new end of yarn, knit the stitch by taking it around the right needle counterclockwise.

4 Slide the right needle down through the stitch on the left needle and under the tail end of yarn. Remove the left needle and allow the stitch to transfer to the right needle.

Intarsia

The term Intarsia comes from the Italian word *intario*, which means "to inlay," and it is used when describing a decorative inlaid pattern in a surface, especially a knitted design featuring areas of differing color that are visible on both sides of the fabric. This technique is used predominantly for motif knitting, where a large area of a second color is required. It creates a single thickness of fabric, and yarns are crossed over each other at specific points in order to change the color sequence without leaving any gaps in the knitted fabric.

Changing Color on a Right-Side Row

1 Work to where the yarn color needs to change. (This will be determined by your chosen pattern.)

2 Take the color that you have finished with *over* the top of the second color to be worked, creating a cross in the yarns.

3 Pick up and begin to work in the new color. The color that you have finished with will stay in its position, and the yarn will hang from the back of your work until you need it again on the following row.

Changing Color on a Wrong-Side Row

1 Work to where the color needs to change.

2 Take the color that you have finished with *over* the top of the second color to be worked, creating a cross in the yarns.

3 Pick up and begin to work in the new color. The color that you have finished with will stay in its position and hang to the front of your work until you need it again on the following row.

Fair Isle

This technique allows a second color to be used in small areas repetitively over each row. It creates a double fabric because yarns are carried on the reverse of the work between each color change. The double fabric is made up of strands of yarn that have been carried across the reverse of the work and the knitted fabric in front of them. Fair Isle is worked over stockinette stitch and features two main techniques, which are known as stranding and weaving in. Stranding is done when the gap between a color change is no more than three stitches; the yarns are carried across the back of the fabric between color changes and knitted in at intervals. Weaving in is done when the gap between a color change is more than three stitches; to avoid large loops of yarn showing on the reverse of the fabric, these strands of yarn need to be caught or woven in on the wrong side of the work.

Stranding on a Right Side Row

This is done when you have a gap of three (or fewer) stitches between a color change.

1 Hold the main color in your right hand and the second color in your left. Keep the tension of the yarn in your left hand by placing the yarn over your index finger. In this example, the next stitch in the row is going to be knitted in the second color which is held in the left hand.

2 Slide the right needle knitwise into the stitch
on the left needle, and pass the second color
over the right needle.

 Bring the yarn through the stitch and slide
from the left needle, transferring it to the
right needle.

Stranding on a Wrong-Side Row

1 Hold the main color in your right hand and the second color under your left thumb. Work to where the color change is required. (Here, stranding will be done across three stitches.) The next stitch in the row is going to be purled, using the second color, which is held in position by the left thumb.

2 Slide the right needle purlwise into the stitch on the left needle.

3 Hold the second color of yarn between the finger and thumb of your left hand and wrap it around the right needle counterclockwise from right to left. This is the same as purling a stitch, only you are using your left hand.

4 Push the new yarn through the stitch from front to back and slide the loop from the left needle, transferring it to the right knitting needle.

Weaving on a Right-Side Row

When there is a gap of more than three stitches between a color change you will need to secure one color on the wrong side of your work in order to avoid getting large floats across the fabric. The yarns are held as for stranding. Weaving in this way is very secure because the yarn being woven is caught by the main color twice, making it hard for the stitches to slip.

1 Hold the main color in your right hand and the second color in the left. Keep the tension of your yarn in your left hand as for stranding. Work to where the second color needs to be woven in. In this example, the yarn in the left hand is going to be caught in on the wrong side of the work.

2 Slide the right needle into the next stitch on the left needle knitwise and, at the same time, pass it under the yarn held in the left hand.

3 Knit the stitch with the main color by wrapping the yarn counterclockwise around the right needle.

4 Holding the second color out of the way, bring the new stitch through to the front, being careful not to bring the yarn that is being woven through to the front also. The purple yarn is not creating a stitch, it is being woven on the wrong side of the work. Do not drop the second color.

5 Knit the next stitch in the main color. This will automatically catch the second color once more. Continue to weave the yarn in on the wrong side of your work until you need to work a stitch (or stitches) in the second color.

Weaving on a Wrong-Side Row

1 Hold the main color in your right hand and the second color under your left thumb. Work to where the second color needs to be woven in.

2 Slide the right needle purlwise into the next stitch on the left needle and, at the same time, pass it *under* the yarn held in the left hand.

3 Purl the stitch with the main color by wrapping the yarn around the right needle from right to left. Bring the second color to the front from behind the right needle and push the main color back through the stitch. The example shows the stitch being purled in the main color and the second color sitting on the facing side, having been caught in once.

4 Hold the second color in place on the facing side of the work and purl the next stitch.

5 Purling the next stitch will automatically catch the second color once more. Do not drop the second color. If you are following a design that requires you to strand more frequently than after three stitches, the technique remains the same.

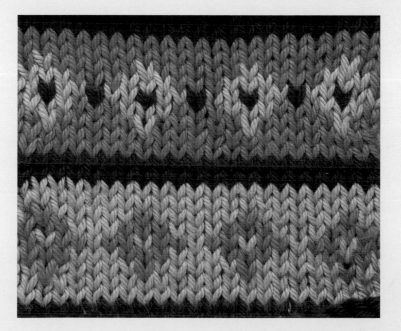

Projects *baby knits*

Denim Bonnet and Bootees

Inspired by retro knitting patterns, this project reinvents the traditional baby bonnet that has been around in knitted form for many years. By accompanying it with cute matching booties, this set will make a great gift for a new baby.

Rowan Denim fades when washed, and its appearance will actually improve with age, making it a great heirloom to be passed from one generation to another.

These projects are suitable for knitters wanting to progress to more complicated shaping techniques without embarking on a large project.

Techniques Used

Casting On

Knitting a Stitch

Purling a Stitch

Knitting Two Stitches Together

Stockinette Stitch

Casting Off

Making a Stitch

Slipping a Stitch

Purling Two Stitches Together

MATERIALS

- 3 (3:3) × 50 g balls Rowan Denim DK
- Pair each of size 3 (3¼ mm) and size 6 (4 mm) needles

MEASUREMENTS

To fit ages: 0–3 3–6 6–12 months

TENSION

Before washing: 20 sts and 28 rows to 4 in. / 10 cm square over st st using size 6 (4 mm) needles

ABBREVIATIONS

See page 15.

Bonnet

MAIN PART

With size 3 (3¼ mm) needles, cast on 74 (80:86) sts.

K 3 rows.

Change to size 6 (4 mm) needles.

Next row K to end.

Next row K2, p to last 2 sts, k2.

Rep the last 2 rows until work measures 2¾ in. (7 cm) from cast-on edge, ending with a p row.

Next row K2 sts, leave these sts on a holder. K to last 2 sts, leave these sts on a holder.

Mark each end of last row with a thread of colored yarn.

Cont in st st, work 3 rows.

Eyelet row K1, * yf, k2 tog; rep from * to last 3 sts, yf, k2 tog, k1.

Work 2 rows in st st.

Next row P to end, k2 sts from holder.

Next row K to end, k2 sts from holder.

Mark each end of last row with a thread of colored yarn.

Starting with a k row cont in st st until work measures 4 (4¼:4¾) in. / 10 (11:12) cm from eyelet row, ending with a k row.

Mark each end of last row with a thread of colored yarn.

Work 3 rows in st st.

Eyelet row K1, * yf, k2 tog; rep from * to last 3 sts, yf, k2 tog, k1.

Work 3 rows in st st.

Mark each end of last row with a thread of colored yarn.

K 2 rows.

Shape crown

Change to size 3 (3¼ mm) needles.

Next row K2, * k2 tog, k4; rep from *
to end. 62 (67:72) sts.

K 5 rows.

Next row K2, * k2 tog, k3; rep from *
to end. 50 (54:58) sts.

K 5 rows.

Next row K2, * k2 tog, k2; rep from *
to end. 38 (41:44) sts.

K 5 rows.

Next row K2, * k2 tog, k1; rep from *
to end. 26 (28:30) sts.

K 5 rows.

Next row K2, * k2 tog; rep from * to end.
14 (15:16) sts.

K 5 rows.

Next row K2 (1:2), * k2 tog; rep from *
to end. 8 (8:9) sts.

K 1 row.

Leaving a long end, cut off yarn and
thread through rem sts. Remove sts
from needle.

EDGING

With right side facing, using size 3 (3¼ mm)
needles, pick up and k21(23:25) sts
along row ends between 2nd and 3rd
threads of colored yarn. Miss crown
section, then pick up and k21(23:25)
sts along row ends between 2nd and 3rd
threads of colored yarn on other side.

K 3 rows.

Cast off.

CHIN STRAPS

Using size 3 (3¼ mm) needles, cast on
40 (45:50) sts.

K 9 (11:13) rows.

Cast off.

TO FINISH

Wash and dry, as indicated on ball band.

Fold along the eyelet row matching colored
markers, and slip stitch rows together to
form picot edging.

Sew seam to beg of crown shaping.
Sew on straps. Weave in yarn ends.

Bootees

(Make two)

With size 3 (3¼ mm) needles cast on
23 (27:31) sts.

Row 1 K to end.

Row 2 K1, m1, k10 (12:14), m1, k1, m1,
k10 (12:14), m1, k1. 27 (31:35) sts.

Row 3 and foll 2 alt rows K to end.

Row 4 K2, m1, k10 (12:14), m1, k3, m1,
k10 (12:14), m1, k2. 31 (35:39) sts

Row 6 K3, m1, k10 (12:14), m1, k5, m1,
k10 (12:14), m1, k3. 35 (39:43) sts.

Row 8 K4, m1, k10 (12:14), m1, k7, m1,
k10 (12:14), m1, k4. 39 (43:47) sts.

Rows 9 and 10 K to end.

Change to size 6 (4 mm) needles.

Starting with a k row, cont in st st.

Work 1 row. Mark each end of this row with
a thread of colored yarn.

Work 3 rows.

Eyelet row K2, * yf, k2 tog; rep from *
to last 3 sts, yf, k2 tog, k1.

Work 3 rows.

Mark each end of last row with a
thread of colored yarn.

Work 6 (8:10) rows in st st.

Shape instep

Row 1 K21 (24:27), skpo, turn.

Row 2 Sl1, p3 (5:7), p2 tog, turn.

Row 3 Sl1, k3 (5:7), skpo, turn.

Rep rows 2 and 3, 3 (4:5) times more, then
row 2 again. 29 (31:33) sts.

Next row Sl1, k to end.

Next row P to end.

Change to size 3 (3¼ mm) needles.

Row 1 K to end.

Row 2 P to end.

Rep the last 2 rows 4 times more and
row 1 again.

Mark each end of last row with a
thread of colored yarn.

Starting with a k row, work 4 rows st st.

Eyelet row K2, * yf, k2 tog; rep from *
to last 3 sts, yf, k2 tog, k1.

Work 3 rows.

Mark each end of last row with a
thread of colored yarn.

Change to size 6 (4 mm) needles.

Work an additional 7 rows in st st.

Change to size 3 (3¼ mm) needles.

K 3 rows in st st.

Cast off.

TO FINISH

Wash and dry, as indicated on ball band.

Fold along the eyelet row matching colored
markers, and slip stitch rows together to
form picot edging.

Sew sole and back seam tog, reversing
seam on cuff. Weave in yarn ends.

Openwork Shawl

A new baby—whether a boy or girl, and no matter how fractious their current temperament—will at least *look* angelic when wrapped in this beautiful shawl. A traditional pattern incorporating openwork stitching, this shawl is knitted from a super-soft, baby-friendly yarn which comes in a huge variety of colors, and is perfect for keeping your precious little one warm, even on the coldest days.

To create a professional finish, make sure that the tassels are uniform in length.

Techniques Used

Techniques Used
Casting On
Knitting a Stitch
Knitting Two Stitches Together
Casting Off

MATERIALS

- 5 × 50 g balls Rowan Calmer
- Pair size 8 (5 mm) needles

MEASUREMENTS

Approx 26 in. / 66 cm square, excluding tassels

TENSION

23 sts and 32 rows to 4 in. / 10 cm square over patt using size 6 (4 mm) needles

ABBREVIATIONS

See page 15.

SHAWL

With size 8 (5 mm) needles, cast on 150 sts.

Row 1 K to end.

Row 2 K1, * yf, k2 tog; rep from * to last st, k1.

Rows 3 to 10 K to end.

These 10 rows form the patt and are repeated throughout.

Cont in patt until work measures 26 in. / 66 cm from cast-on edge, ending with row 3. Cast off.

TO FINISH

Cut remaining yarn into 5½ in. / 14 cm lengths and knot seven together through each eyelet along side edges and alternate eyelets along top and bottom edges. Weave in yarn ends.

Four-Piece Cashmere Set

A pull-on hat is a must for all stylish babies, mitts are much warmer than conventional mittens, and the toasty bootees are perfect for tiny feet. The matching cardigan can be worn throughout the year and completes the look. All pieces are worked in a luxurious cashmere-and-wool-mix yarn in stockinette stitch and rib and have a contrast cuff. Experiment with color combinations to create a striking set.

Techniques Used

Casting On
Knitting a Stitch
Purling a Stitch
Joining in a New Color
Double Rib
Slipping a Stitch
Stockinette Stitch
Casting Off
Making a Stitch
Knitting Two Stitches Together

MATERIALS

Cardigan

- 2 (3:3) × 50 g balls of Rowan Cashsoft Baby DK in Cream (M)
- 1 (1:2) × 50 g ball(s) in Green (C)
- Pair each size 3 (3¼ mm) and size 6 (4 mm) needles
- 5 buttons

Hat, Mitts, and Bootees

- 2 (2:3) × 50 g balls of Rowan Cashsoft Baby DK in Cream (M)
- 1 (1:2) × 50 g ball(s) in Green (C)
- Pair each size 3 (3¼ mm) and size 6 (4 mm) needles

CARDIGAN MEASUREMENTS

Age (in months)		
0–3	3–6	6–12
Chest		
20	22	24 in.
51	56	61 cm
Length		
9½	10¼	11 in.
24	26	28 cm
Sleeve		
5½	6¾	8 in.
14	17	20 cm

TENSION

22 sts and 30 rows to 4 in. / 10 cm square over st st using size 6 (4 mm) needles

ABBREVIATIONS

See page 15.

Cardigan BACK and FRONT worked in one piece

With size 3 (3¼ mm) needles and C, cast on 112 (124:136) sts.

Row 1 K3, * p2, k2; rep from * to last 5 sts, p2, k3.

Row 2 P3, * k2, p2; rep from * to last 3 sts, k2, p3.

Rep the last 2 rows 3 times more.

Change to size 6 (4 mm) needles.

Beg with a k, row cont in st st and stripes of 10 rows M and 2 rows C until work measures 5 (5½:6) in. / 13 (14:15) cm from cast-on edge, ending with a p row.

Divide for armholes

Next row K27 (30:33), turn and work on these sts for right front.

Work 5 rows straight.

Shape neck

Next row K1, skpo, k to end.

Next row P to end.

Rep the last 2 rows 6 (7:8) times more. 20 (22:24) sts.

Work straight until work measures 9½ (10¼:11) in. / 24 (26:28) cm from cast-on edge, ending with a p row.

Cast off.

Back

With rs facing, rejoin yarn to rem sts, k58 (64:70), turn and work on these sts for back.

Cont straight until work measures 9½ (10¼:11) in. / 24 (26:28) cm from cast-on edge, ending with a p row.

Shape shoulders

Cast off 20 (22:24) sts at beg of next 2 rows.

Leave rem 18 (20:22) sts on a holder.

Left front

With right side facing, rejoin yarn to rem sts, k to end. 27 (30:33) sts.

Work 5 rows straight.

Shape neck

Next row K to last 3 sts, k2 tog, k1.

Next row P to end.

Rep the last 2 rows 6 (7:8) times more. 20 (22:24) sts.

Work straight until work measures 9½ (10¼:11) in. / 24 (26:28) cm from cast-on edge, ending with a p row.

Cast off.

SLEEVES (Make two)

With size 3 (3¼ mm) needles and C, cast on 30 (34:38) sts.

Row 1 K2, * p2, k2; rep from * to end.

Row 2 P2, * k2, p2; rep from * to end.

Rep last 2 rows 3 more times.

Change to size 6 (4 mm) needles.

Beg with a k row, cont in st st and stripes of 10 rows M and 2 rows C at the same time.

Shape sleeves as follows:

Work 2 rows.

Inc row K3, m1, k to last 3 sts, m1, k3.

Starting with a p row, work 5 rows in st st.

Rep the last 6 rows until there are 40 (46:52) sts.

Cont straight until sleeve measures 5½ (6¾:8) in. / 14 (17:20) cm from cast-on edge, ending with a p row. Cast off.

FRONT BAND

Sew shoulder seams tog.

With right side facing, using size 3 (3¼ mm) needles and C, pick up and k58 (63:68) sts up right front to shoulder, k across 18 (20:22) sts from holder, pick up and k58 (63:68) sts down left front. 134 (146:158) sts.

Row 1 P2, * k2, p2; rep from * to end.

Row 2 K2, * p2, k2; rep from * to end.

These 2 rows form the rib.

Work 1 more row.

Buttonhole row Rib 2, [rib 2 tog, yf, rib 6 (7:8) sts] 4 times, rib 2 tog, yf, rib to end.

Rib 3 rows.

Cast off in rib

TO FINISH

Sew sleeve seams tog. Sew in sleeves. Sew on buttons. Weave in yarn ends.

Hat

With size 6 (4 mm) needles and C, cast on 82 (90:98) sts.

Row 1 K2, * p2, k2; rep from * to end.

Row 2 P2, * k2, p2; rep from * to end.

Rep the last 2 rows 5 (6:6) times more.

Change to size 3 (3¼ mm) needles.

Work a further 12 (14:14) more rows in rib.

Change to size 6 (4 mm) needles and M.

Starting with a k row, work 12 (14:16) rows.

Shape crown

Row 1 [K8 (9:10), k2 tog] 8 times, k2.

Row 2 P to end. 74 (82:90) sts.

Row 3 [K7 (8:9), k2 tog] 8 times, k2.

Row 4 P to end. 66 (74:82) sts.

Row 5 [K6 (7:8), k2 tog] 8 times, k2.

Row 6 P to end. 58 (66:74) sts.

Row 7 [K5 (6:7), k2 tog] 8 times, k2.

Row 8 P to end. 50 (58:66) sts.

Row 9 [K4 (5:6), k2 tog] 8 times, k2. 42 (50:58) sts.

Row 10 P to end.

Row 11 [K3 (4:5), k2 tog] 8 times, k2.

Row 12 P to end.

Row 13 [K2 (3:4), k2 tog] 8 times, k2. 34 (42:50) sts.

Row 14 P to end.

Row 15 [K1 (2:3), k2 tog] 8 times, k2. 26 (34:42) sts.

Row 16 P to end.

2nd and 3rd sizes only

Row 17 [K (1:2), k2 tog] 8 times, k2. 26 (26:26) sts.

Row 18 P to end.

3rd size only

Row 19 [K (1), k2 tog] 8 times, k2. 26 (26:34) sts.

Row 20 P to end.

All sizes

Next row [K2 tog] 9 times.

Leaving a long end, cut off yarn and thread through rem sts. Pull up and secure, and remove sts from needle.

TO FINISH

Sew seam, reversing seam on brim. Weave in yarn ends.

Mitts

(Make two)

With size 6 (4 mm) needles and C, cast on 26 (30:34) sts.

Row 1 K2, * p2, k2; rep from * to end.

Row 2 P2, * k2, p2; rep from * to end.

Rep the last 2 rows 3 (4:4) more times.

Change to size 3 (3¼ mm) needles.

Work 8 (10:10) more rows in rib.

Cut off C.

Change to size 6 (4 mm) needles and M.

Starting with a k row, work 14 (18,20) rows in st st.

Shape top

Row 1 K2, [skpo, k6 (8:10), k2tog, k2] twice.

Row 2 P to end.

Row 3 K2, [skpo, k4 (6:8), k2tog, k2] twice.

Row 4 P to end. Cast off.

TO FINISH

Sew seam, reversing seam on cuff. Weave in yarn ends.

Bootees

(Make two)

With size 3 (3¼ mm) needles and M cast on 23 (27:31) sts.

Row 1 K to end.

Row 2 K1, m1, k10 (12:14), m1, k1, m1, k10 (12:14), m1, k1. 27 (31:35) sts.

Row 3 and 2 foll alt rows K to end.

Row 4 K2, m1, k10 (12:14), m1, k3, m1, k10 (12:14), m1, k2. 31 (35:39) sts.

Row 6 K3, m1, k10 (12:14), m1, k5, m1, k10 (12:14), m1, k3. 35 (39:43) sts.

Row 8 K4, m1, k10 (12:14), m1, k7, m1, k10 (12:14), m1, k4. 39 (43:47) sts.

Change to size 6 (4 mm) needles.

Starting with a k row, work 8 (10:10) rows in st st.

Shape instep

Row 1 K23 (26:29), skpo, turn.

Row 2 Sl1, p7 (9:11), p2 tog, turn.

Row 3 Sl1, k7 (9:11), skpo, turn.

Rep rows 2 and 3, 3 (4:5) times more, then row 2 again.

Next row Sl1, k to end.

Next row P14 (7:16), m1, [p0 (8:0), m1] 0 (2:0) times, p15 (8:17). 30 (34:34) sts.

Change to size 3 (3¼ mm) needles and C.

Row 1 K to end.

Row 2 K2, * p2, k2; rep from * to end.

Row 3 P2, * k2, p2; rep from * to end.

Rep the last 2 rows 3 more times.

Change to size 6 (4 mm) needles.

Work an additional 10 rows in rib.

Cast off in rib.

TO FINISH

Join sole and back seam, reversing seam on cuff. Weave in yarn ends.

Play Pillow

Knitted in eye-catching colors, this cute bolster pillow will make a great toy for babies beginning to explore the world around them. Designed for the 6-to-12 month age range, this baby roll will not only provide support to those learning to sit but will also provide hours of fun.

There is a zipper that can be unfastened, a Velcro® panel that will stick back into place, and a cord detail that encourages children to learn to tie.

The two round end panels are knitted separately, and then the roll is put together with only one main seam.

Techniques Used

Casting On

Stockinette Stitch

Joining in a New Color

Knitting Two Stitches Together

Knitting a Stitch

Purling a Stitch

Casting Off

MATERIALS

- 1 x 50 g ball each of Rowan Handknit Cotton in Red (A), Orange (B), Yellow (C) Green (D), Light Blue (E), Dark Blue (F), and Purple (G)
- Pair of size 6 (4 mm) needles
- Two size 6 (4 mm) double-pointed needles
- Bolster pillow pad 16 in. / 41 cm long and 20 in. / 51 cm round
- 6 in. / 15 cm chunky zipper
- One large button
- 2 in. / 5 cm red Velcro®

MEASUREMENTS

Approx 16 in. / 41cm long and 20 in. / 51cm round

TENSION

20 sts and 28 rows to 4 in. / 10 cm square over st st using size 6 (4 mm) needles

ABBREVIATIONS

See page 15.

PLAY PILLOW

Main part

With size 6 (4 mm) needles and A, cast on 80 sts.

Cont in st st and stripes of 2 rows A, B, C, D, E, F, and G.

These 14 rows form the stripe sequence.

Work an additional 126 rows.

Cast off.

End pieces (Make two)

With rs facing, using size 6 (4 mm) needles and A, pick up and K 109 sts along row ends.

Cont in stripe sequence as given for main part.

Row 1 P to end.

Row 2 [K10, k2 tog] 9 times, k1.

Row 3 and every foll alt row P to end.

Row 4 [K9, k2 tog] 9 times, k1.

Row 6 [K8, k2 tog] 9 times, k1.

Row 8 [K7, k2 tog] 9 times, k1.

Row 10 [K6, k2 tog] 9 times, k1.

Row 12 [K5, k2 tog] 9 times, k1.

Row 14 [K4, k2 tog] 9 times, k1.

Row 16 [K3, k2 tog] 9 times, k1.

Row 18 [K2, k2 tog] 9 times, k1.

Row 20 [K1, k2 tog] 9 times, k1.

Row 22 [K2 tog] 9 times, k1.

Row 23 [P2 tog] 5 times.

Leaving a long end, cut off yarn and thread through rem sts. Pull up and secure, and remove sts from needle.

Starting and finishing at center of end pieces sew seam, placing bolster pillow inside.

ZIPPED PANEL

First side

With size 6 (4 mm) needles and G, cast on 8 sts.

Row 1 K to end.

Row 2 K2, p to end.

Rep these 2 rows 27 times more.

Cast off.

Second side

With size 6 (4 mm) needles and G, cast on 8 sts.

Row 1 K to end.

Row 2 P6, k2.

Rep these 2 rows 27 times more. Cast off.

To Finish

With g st cdgings together, sew first 10 rows and last 4 rows.

Sew in zipper.

Sew all four sides to roll securely. Weave in yarn ends.

VELCRO® PANEL

With size 6 (4 mm) needles and A, cast on 8 sts.

Row 1 * K1, p1; rep from * to end.

Row 2 * P1, k1; rep from * to end.

Rep these 2 rows 16 times more.

Cast off.

To Finish

Sew cast-off edge to roll, then sew one half of the Velcro to end of back of knitted tab. Sew other piece of Velcro to roll.

BUTTONED PANEL

With size 6 (4 mm) needles and D, cast on 16 sts.

Row 1 K to end.

Row 2 K to end.

Row 3 K2, p to last 2 sts, k2.

Rep the last 2 rows 4 times more.

Buttonhole row 1 K4, cast off 8 sts, k to end.

Buttonhole row 2 K2, p2, cast on 8 sts, p next st, k2.

Rep rows 2 and 3, 10 times more.

Cast off.

To Finish

Sew cast-off edge to roll. Sew on button to correspond with buttonhole. Weave in yarn ends.

LACED PANEL

First side

With size 6 (4 mm) needles and C, cast on 11 sts.

Row 1 K to end.

Row 2 P9, k2.

Rep these 2 rows once more.

**Buttonhole row 1 K3, cast off 3 sts, k to end.

Buttonhole row 2 P5, cast on 3 sts, k ext 2 sts.

Rep rows 1 and 2 four times.

Rep from ** four times more.

**Buttonhole row 1 K3, cast off 3 sts, k to end.

Buttonhole row 2 P5, p3, cast on 3 sts, k ext 2 sts.

Rep rows 1 and 2 twice.

K 5 rows.

Cast off.

Second side

With size 6 (4 mm) needles and C, cast on 11 sts.

Row 1 K to end.

Row 2 K2, p9.

Rep these 2 rows once more.

**Buttonhole row 1 K5, cast off 3 sts, k to end.

Buttonhole row 2 K2, p1, cast on 3 sts, k2, p to end.

Rep rows 1 and 2 four times.

Rep from ** four times more.

**Buttonhole row 1 K5, cast off 3 sts, k to end.

Buttonhole row 2 K2, p1, cast on 3 sts, p to end.

Rep rows 1 and 2 twice.

K 5 rows.

Cast off.

Lace

Using size 6 (4 mm) double-pointed needles cast on 3 sts.

Row 1 [Inc in next st] 3 times. 6 sts, do not turn, bring yarn across back of work to beginning of row.

Row 2 K to end, do not turn, bring yarn across back of work to beginning of row.

Rep row 2 until tie measures 39 in. / 100 cm.

Work [2tog] 3 times, thread yarn through remaining sts and fasten off.

To Finish

With g st edgings together, sew first 2 rows. Thread the lace through the buttonholes. Attach to pillow along cast-on and side edges. Weave in yarn ends.

Baby Jacket and Bootees

Knitting for babies is a great way for the new knitter to learn
techniques such as shaping and textured stitches, without having
to embark on a large project. This lovely set is ideal for a newborn
and would make a beautiful present for a baby shower.

    Knitted in a soft cotton-mix yarn there is very little shaping
in the cardigan and the bootees, so you can concentrate
on achieving an even gauge over seed stitch. For any garment,
it is a good idea to sew a spare button onto the inside seam.

Techniques Used

Casting On

Knitting a Stitch

Purling a Stitch

Seed Stitch

Casting Off

Slipping a Stitch

Knitting Two Stitches Together

MATERIALS

- 3 × 50 g balls Rowan Calmer
- Pair size 7 (4½ mm) needles
- 4 buttons

MEASUREMENTS

To fit 0-to-3 months

Jacket

Actual measurements

Chest 19¾ in. / 50 cm

Length to shoulder 10½ in. / 27 cm

Sleeve length 6 in. / 15 cm

TENSION

24 sts and 43 rows to 4 in. / 10 cm square over seed st using size 7 (4½ mm) needles

ABBREVIATIONS

See page 15.

Jacket

BACK

With size 7 (4½ mm) needles, cast on 62 sts.

K 3 rows.

Seed st row 1(rs) * K1, p1; rep from * to end.

Seed st row 2 * P1, k1; rep from * to end.

These 2 rows form the seed st and are repeated throughout.

Work straight until back measures 10½ in. / 27 cm. from cast-on edge, ending with a ws row.

Cast off.

LEFT FRONT

With size 7 (4½ mm) needles, cast on 34 sts.

K 3 rows.

Working buttonholes for boy (see box, above), cont in seed st as given for back until front measures 6¼ in. / 16 cm from cast-on edge, ending with seed st row 2.

Shape neck

Next row Patt to last 4 sts, work 2 tog, patt 2.

Work 3 rows straight.

Rep the last 4 rows until 22 sts rem.

Work straight until front matches back to shoulder, ending at side edge. Cast off.

RIGHT FRONT

With size 7 (4½ mm) needles, cast on 34 sts.

K 3 rows.

Working buttonholes for girl (see box, above), cont in seed st as given for back until front measures 6¼ in. / 16 cm from cast-on edge, ending with seed st row 2.

Shape neck

Next row Patt 2, work 2 tog, patt to end.

Work 3 rows straight.

Rep the last 4 rows until 22 sts rem.

Work straight until front matches back to shoulder, ending at side edge.

Cast off.

SLEEVES

With size 7 (4½ mm) needles, cast on 32 sts.

K 30 rows.

Cont in seed st **at the same time** inc one st at each end of the first and every foll 8th row until there are 46 sts.

Work straight until work measures 7½ in. / 19 cm from cast-on edge.

Cast off.

TO FINISH

Sew shoulder seams tog. Sew on sleeves. Sew side and sleeve seams. Weave in yarn ends.

Sew on buttons. Turn back cuffs.

Bootees

(Make two)

With size 7 (4½ mm) needles, cast on 40 sts.

K 22 rows.

Cast off 9 sts at beg of next 2 rows. 22 sts.

K 8 rows.

Shape for toes

Next row K9, skpo, k2 tog, k9.

Next row K8, skpo, k2 tog, k8.

Next row K7, skpo, k2 tog, k7.

Cont in this way, decreasing 2 sts on every row until 4 sts rem.

Next row K1, k2 tog, k1.

K3 tog and fasten off.

TO FINISH

Sew short seam to cast-off edge. Sew back seam, reversing seam on last 8 sts for cuff. Weave in yarn ends.

Turn back cuffs.

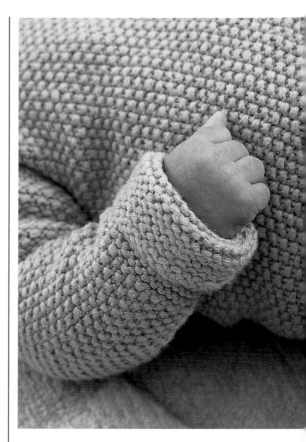

Seed Stitch Crib Blanket

Large items such as shawls, blankets, and crib covers can be particularly daunting to beginner knitters. This one, however, is simple in design and is knitted using a chunky, soft cotton yarn, making it quick and easy to knit.

Worked in seed stitch, the yarn color is changed every few rows to create attractive stripes.

The blanket could be used as a play mat for a small baby, or to cover the baby carriage when out and about, and its soothing colors make it appealing to the very young.

Techniques Used

Casting On

Knitting a Stitch

Purling a Stitch

Seed Stitch

Joining in a New Color

Casting Off

MATERIALS

- 3 × 50 g balls of Rowan Calmer in Blue
- 2 × balls each Cream and Green
- Pair of size 11 (8 mm) needles

MEASUREMENTS

23 in. / 58 cm wide by 26¾ in. / 68 cm long

ABBREVIATIONS

See page 15.

TENSION

14 sts and 25 rows to 4 in. / 10 cm square over seed st, using size 11 (8 mm) needles and yarn used double

NOTE

Use yarn double throughout.

Do not break off yarn after each stripe, but twist it neatly up the side of work, so that it is ready to use when next required.

CRIB BLANKET

With size 11 (8 mm) needles and Green, cast on 75 sts.

Patt row K1, * p1, k1; rep from * to end.

Rep this row to form the seed st pattern.

Work 1 more row.

Now work in stripes of 3 rows Cream, 3 rows Blue, and 3 rows Green.

Cont in patt until blanket measures 24¾ in. / 63 cm, ending with 2 rows in Cream.

Using Cream, cast off in patt.

Side Edgings

With rs facing, size 11 (8 mm) needles, and Blue, pick up and k97 sts along row ends.

Work 6 rows seed st, increasing 1st at each end of the 2nd, 4th, and 6th rows.

Cast off in seed st.

Top and Bottom Edgings

With rs facing, size 11 (8 mm) needles and Blue, pick up and k73 sts along each edge.

Work 6 rows in seed st, increasing 1 st at each end of the 2nd, 4th, and 6th rows.

Cast off in seed st.

TO FINISH

Sew mitered corners. Weave in yarn ends.

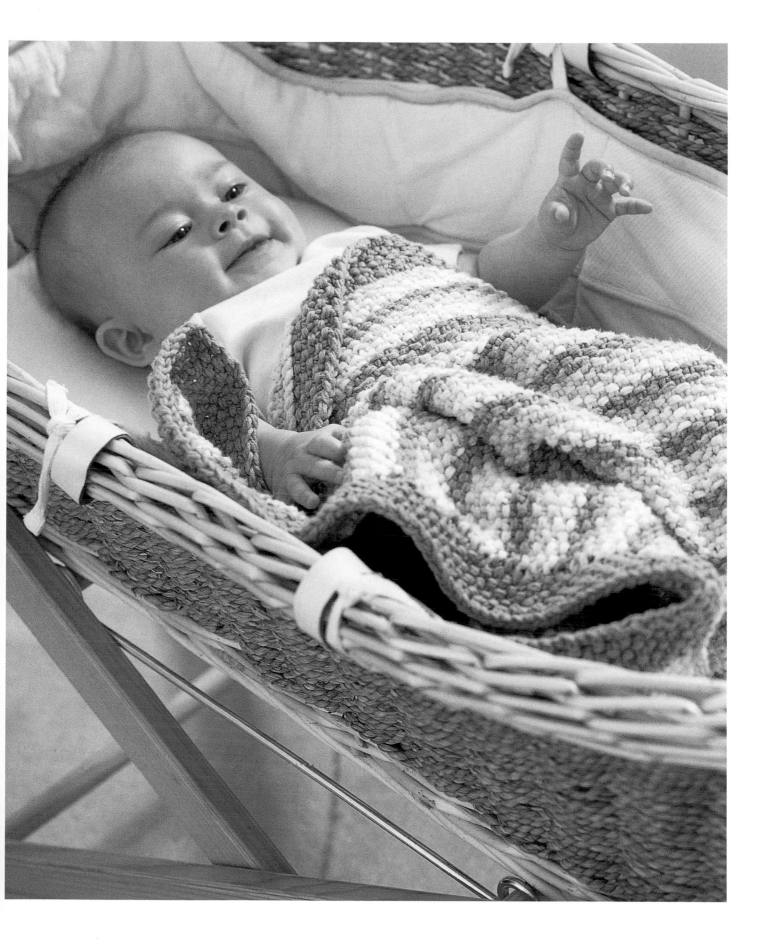

Baby Beret and Bootees

Knitted using a machine-washable wool/cotton mix yarn, these garter stitch bootees with a matching beret would make a great addition to a baby's layette.

Garter stitch is made by working only knit stitches on every row (*see* page 26) and is the easier of the two stitches that make up a knitted fabric.

These projects both feature garter stitch and basic shaping techniques. They are a great introduction to the world of knitting, and are relatively quick to complete.

Techniques Used

Casting On

Knitting a Stitch

Purling a Stitch

Double Rib

Making a Stitch

Knitting Two Stitches Together

Garter Stitch

Slipping a Stitch

Casting Off

MATERIALS

- 2 (2:3) × 50 g balls of Rowan Wool/ Cotton DK
- Pair each of size 3 (3¼ mm) and size 5 (3¾ mm) needles

MEASUREMENTS

To fit ages: 0–3 3–6 6–12 months

TENSION

23 sts and 37 rows to 4 in. / 10 cm square over garter st using size 5 (3¾ mm) needles

ABBREVIATIONS

See page 15.

Beret

With size 3 (3¼ mm) needles, cast on 78 (82:86) sts.

Rib row 1 K2, * p2, k2; rep from * to end.

Rib row 2 P2, * k2, p2; rep from * to end.

Rep the last 2 rows once more.

Change to size 5 (3¾ mm) needles. K2 rows.

Next row K2, [m1, k2] 38 (40:42) times. K 3 rows. 116 (122:128) sts.

Next row K2, [m1, k3] 38 (40:42) times. 154 (162:170) sts.

K 17 (19:21) rows.

Shape crown

Row 1 [K17 (18:19), k2 tog] 8 times, k2.

Row 2 K to end.

Row 3 [K16 (17:18), k2 tog] 8 times, k2.

Row 4 K to end.

Row 5 [K15 (16:17), k2 tog] 8 times, k2.

Row 6 K to end.

Row 7 [K14 (15:16), k2 tog] 8 times, k2.

Row 8 K to end.

Row 9 [K13 (14:15), k2 tog] 8 times, k2.

Row 10 K to end.

Row 11 [K12 (13:14), k2 tog] 8 times, k2.

Row 12 K to end.

Row 13 [K11 (12:13), k2 tog] 8 times, k2.

Row 14 K to end.

Cont in this way, working 8 decs on every alt row until 18 sts rem.

Next row K to end.

Next row [K2 tog] 9 times.

Leaving a long end, cut off yarn and thread through rem sts. Pull up and secure.

TO FINISH

Sew seam. Weave in yarn ends.

Bootees

(Make two)

With size 5 (3¾ mm) needles cast on 24 (28:32) sts.

Work in garter st until work measures 3 (3¼:3½) in. / 8 (8½:9) cm from cast-on edge.

Shape instep

Next row (rs) K15 (18:21), turn.

Next row K6 (8:10), turn.

Cont in garter st on 6 (8:10) sts until instep measures 1⅛ (1¼:1½) in. / 3 (3.5:4) cm, ending with a ws row.

Break off yarn.

With right side facing, rejoin yarn at base of instep and pick up and k7 (9:11) sts along side of instep, k across center 6 (8:10) sts, then pick up and k7 (9:11) sts along other side of instep, k rem 9 (10:11) sts. 38 (46:54) sts.

K 11 rows.

Shape sole

Next row K22 (27:32) sts, turn, leaving rem 16 (19:22) sts unworked.

Next row K6 (8:10) sts, turn, leaving rem 16 (19:22) sts unworked.

Next row K7 (8:9), skpo, turn.

Next row K7 (8:9), k2 tog, turn.

Rep the last 2 rows until 2 (3:4) sts rem unworked at each side.

Turn after last row and k to end.

Cast off.

TO FINISH

Sew back seam, reversing seam on last half of cuff. With back seam to center of sole, sew heel seam. Weave in yarn ends.

Projects *kid knits*

Rainbow Poncho and Hat

The poncho is a fashionable must among women and young girls—this design is inspired by traditional Andean ponchos, which are renowned for their bright colors.

The accompanying hat is great for small children on a cold day! The earflaps are knitted separately and held on a spare needle and then joined to the hat while casting on the bottom edge.

This is a wonderful project for new knitters; it teaches simple color changes, shaping, and how to hold stitches.

Techniques Used

| Casting On |
| Knitting a Stitch |
| Joining in a New Color |
| Slipping a Stitch |
| Knitting Two Stitches Together |
| Stockinette Stitch |
| Making a Stitch |

MATERIALS

- 8 (10) × 50 g balls of Rowan Handknit Cotton in Navy Blue
- One ball each of Red, Orange, Yellow, Green, Blue and Purple
- Pair each of size 5 (3¾ mm) and size 6 (4 mm) knitting needles

PONCHO MEASUREMENTS

Age (in years)	
6-8	**8-10**
Length (from neck to wrist)	
14½	16½ in.
36	42 cm

Hat

To fit an average child's head

TENSION

20 sts and 28 rows to 4 in. / 10 cm square over st st using size 6 (4 mm) needles

ABBREVIATIONS

See page 15.

Poncho

MAKE 2 PIECES ALIKE

With size 5 (3¾ mm) needles and Navy cast on 149 (165) sts.

Row 1 K to end.

Row 2 K1, skpo, k to last 3 sts, k2 tog, k1.

Row 3 K to end.

Change to size 6 (4 mm) needles.

Beg with a k row cont in st st and patt, as folls:

Row 1 K1, skpo, k to last 3 sts, k2tog, k1.

Row 2 P to end.

Rep the last 2 rows 12 (16) more times.

Cont in stripes of 3 rows each of Red, Orange, Yellow, Green, Navy, Blue, and Purple; **at the same time** cont to dec on every right side row, as before.

Cont in Navy, decreasing as before until 51 sts rem.

Change to size 5 (3¾ mm) needles.

Next row K1, skpo, k to last 3 sts, k2 tog, k1. 49 sts

Eyelet row K3, [k2 tog, yf, k8] 4 times, k2 tog, yf, k4.

K 2 rows.

Cast off.

TO FINISH

Sew center-front and back seams together. Weave in yarn ends.

Cord: Cut 4 x 6½ yd / 6 m lengths in red. Knot the strands together at each end. Hook one knotted end over a door handle, and insert a needle through the other end. Twist the needle clockwise until the strands are tightly twisted. Holding the cord in the center with one hand, bring the knotted ends together and let the two halves twist together. Knot the cut ends together and trim. Knot the folded end and cut the end.

Thread twisted cord through eyelets to tie at center front.

Hat

EAR FLAPS (make 2)

With size 6 (4 mm) needles and Navy, cast on 6 sts.

Next row K to end.

Next row K2, m1, k to last 2 sts, m1, k2.

Next row K to end.

Next row K2, m1, k to last 2 sts, m1, k2.

Next row K2, m1pw, p to last 2 sts, m1pw, k2.

Next row K2, m1, k to last 2 sts, m1, k2.

Next row K2, p to last 2 sts, k2.

Rep the last 2 rows three more times. 20 sts.

Next row K to end.

Next row K2, p to last 2 sts, k2.

Rep the last 2 rows five more times.

Leave these sts on a spare needle or holder.

MAIN PART

With a spare size 6 (4 mm) needle and Navy, cast on 13 sts. Break off yarn; then onto same needle, cast on another 31 sts. Break off yarn.

With size 6 (4 mm) needles, cast on 13 sts. K 13 sts; then k 20 sts of one ear flap, k31 sts from spare needle; then k 20 sts of second ear flap; then k13 sts from spare needle. 97 sts.

Next row K15, p16, k35, p16, k15.

Next row K to end.

Next row K15, p16, k35, p16, k15.

Cont in st st and stripes of 3 rows each of Navy, Red, Orange, Yellow, Green, Navy, Blue and Purple.

Starting in Navy, work 2 rows.

Dec row K2, * k2 tog, k3, k2 tog, k2; rep from * to last 5 sts, k2 tog, k3. 76 sts.

Work 9 rows.

Dec row K1, * k2 tog, k1; rep from * to end. 51 sts.

Work 5 rows.

Dec row K1, * k2 tog; rep from * to end. 26 sts.

Work 5 rows.

Dec row * K2 tog; rep from * to end. 13 sts.

Work 5 more rows.

Cut off yarn thread through rem sts, pull up and secure, and remove sts from needle.

TO FINISH

Join back seam. Weave in yarn ends.

Cut 40 in. / 110 cm Red, and make 2 twisted cords 10½ in. / 27 cm long. Knot one through center of cast-on edge of each ear flap.

Ribbon-Twist Tasseled Scarf

A brilliant first project for any new knitter, this bright, chunky scarf is knitted in garter stitch (which means you knit every row) and has tied-on tassels at each end.

Cut the tassels first, then knit the scarf until you only have enough yarn left to complete the cast off—you won't waste one inch of yarn!

Garter stitch looks the same on both sides, so you don't even have to worry about which side of the work is facing you.

Techniques Used

Casting On

Garter Stitch

Casting Off

MATERIALS

- 3 × 100 g balls of Rowan Ribbon Twist
- Pair of size 17 (12 mm) needles

MEASUREMENTS

8 in. / 20 cm wide by 59 in. / 150 cm long, excluding fringing

TENSION

8 sts and 11 rows to 4 in. / 10 cm square over garter st using size 17 (12 mm) needles

ABBREVIATIONS

See page 15.

SCARF

FRINGING

Cut 64 lengths of yarn 21½ in. / 55 cm long.

MAIN PIECE

With size 17 (12 mm) needles cast on 16 sts.

Leaving enough yarn to cast off, cont in garter st (every row k) until remaining yarn has been used.

Cast off.

TO FINISH

Knot 2 lengths of pre-cut yarn into each st along cast-on and cast-off edges to form fringing. Weave in yarn ends

Rainbow Toy Bag

This project provides a great introduction to intarsia and simple color changing, once you have mastered the basic techniques.

Drawstring bags such as this one are extremely practical, both for young children and moms, and could be used to store toys, or carry gym clothes. The drawstring along the top ensures that the contents remain safe.

The bag is a simple rectangle shape sewn together on three sides. There is a small hem along the top, with a knitted drawstring.

Techniques Used

Casting On

Stockinette Stitch

Joining in a New Color

Knitting Two Stitches Together

Intarsia Color Work

Casting Off

MATERIALS

- 1 × 50 g ball Rowan Cotton DK in each of seven colours Green (A), Orange (B), Purple (C), Red (D), Light Blue (E), Yellow (F), and Bright Blue (G)
- One pair size 6 (4 mm) needles
- Two size 6 (4 mm) double pointed needles

MEASUREMENTS

Approx 13¾ in. / 35 cm wide by 15¼ in. / 39 cm long

TENSION

20 sts and 28 rows to 4 in. / 10 cm square over st st using size 6 (4 mm) needles

ABBREVIATIONS

See page 15.

NOTE

When working motifs, use separate balls of yarn for each area of color. To avoid gaps in your work, twist yarns together on ws, when changing color.

To work Intarsia, see page 50.

BACK

With size 6 (4 mm) needles and A, cast on 70 sts.

Starting with a k row, cont in st st.

Rows 1 to 4 Work 4 rows st st.

Row 5 K8A, 8G, 54A.

Row 6 P54A, 8G, 8A.

Rows 7 to 16 Rep rows 5 and 6 five times.

Rows 17 to 20 Using A work 4 rows st st.

Break off A.

Join in B.

Rows 21 to 24 Work 4 rows st st.

Row 25 K42B, 8E, 20B.

Row 26 P20B, 8E, 42B.

Rows 27 to 36 Rep rows 25 and 26 five times.

Rows 37 to 40 Using B work 4 rows st st.

Break off B.

Join in C.

Rows 41 to 44 Work 4 rows st st.

Row 45 K26C, 8F, 36C.

Row 46 P36C, 8F, 26C.

Rows 47 to 56 Rep rows 45 and 46 five times.

Rows 57 to 60 Using C work 4 rows st st.

Break off C.

Join in D.

Rows 61 to 64 Work 4 rows st st.

Row 65 K6D, 8A, 56D.

Row 66 P56D, 8A, 6D.

Rows 67 to 76 Rep rows 65 and 66 five times.

Rows 77 to 80 Using D work 4 rows st st.

Break off D.

Join in E.

Rows 81 to 84 Work 4 rows st st.

Row 85 K22E, 8C, 40E.

Row 86 P40E, 8C, 22E.

No crops

Rows 87 to 96 Rep rows 85 and 86 five times.

Rows 97 to 100 Using E work 4 rows st st.

Break off E.

Join in F.

Rows 101 to 120 Using E, work 20 rows st st.

Cast off.

FRONT

With right side facing, using size 6 (4 mm) needles and A, pick up and k 70 sts along cast-on edge of back—this counts as row 1.

Starting with row 2, work as given for Back to end.

CORD

Using size 6 (4 mm) double-pointed needles and G, cast on 3 sts.

1st row [Inc in next st] 3 times. 6 sts, do not turn, bring yarn across back of work to beginning of row.

2nd row K to end, do not turn, bring yarn across back of work to beginning of row.

Rep this row until strap measures 33 in. / 84 cm.

Work [2tog] 3 times, thread yarn through remaining sts and fasten off.

TO FINISH

Sew one side seam all the way up to the cast-off edge. Sew other side seam to row 100. Fold last 20 rows in half to ws and stitch in place to form channel. Thread cord through channel and join ends. Weave in yarn ends.

Using a contrasting color, embroider "stitches" around "patches."

Chunky Rainbow Scarf Set

Make a real fashion statement with this mother-and-child matching scarf set!

The scarves feature a very simple lace pattern which has just a four-row repeat. You could use a row counter to keep track of where you are in the pattern, but after a few repeats you will be able to remember the pattern easily.

It is always a good idea to complete a whole repeat before putting your knitting down; however, if this is not possible, make a note of which row you are on so that you don't lose track. The stitch pattern is exactly the same for both scarves—the numbers and measurements in parentheses are for the ladies version.

Knitted in a bright chunky yarn, these scarves will definitely make an impact.

Techniques Used

Casting On

Knitting a Stitch

Purling a Stitch

Purling Two Stitches Together

Casting Off

MATERIALS

- 2 (3) × 100 g balls of Rowan Chunky Print
- Pair of size 11 (8 mm) needles

MEASUREMENTS

Child's scarf 4¾ in. / 12 cm wide by 34 in. / 87 cm long

Adult's scarf 6½ in. / 16½ cm wide by 72 in. / 184 cm long

TENSION

18 sts and 20 rows to 4 in. / 10 cm square over rib patt using size 11 (8 mm) needles

ABBREVIATIONS

See page 15.

SCARF

With size 11 (8 mm) needles, cast on 22 (30) sts.

Rib row 1 (right side) K2, * p2tog, yrn, k2; rep from * to end.

Rib row 2 P2, * k2, p2; rep from * to end.

Rib row 3 K2, * yrn, p2tog, k2; rep from * to end.

Rib row 4 P2, * k2, p2; rep from * to end.

These 4 rows form the patt and are rep throughout.

Leaving enough yarn to cast off, cont to end of 1st (3rd) ball, ending with a rs row. Cast off in rib.

TO FINISH

Weave in yarn ends.

Striped Rib Hat and Scarf

Youngsters look great in bright, unusual colors, as this set demonstrates to great effect.

This scarf and hat set is knitted in a soft wool/cotton mix that is machine washable and will provide a high level of warmth.

The scarf is a good project for learning how to keep ribbing neat and even, while the hat provides a great lesson in shaping and changing color.

Techniques Used

Casting On

Knitting a Stitch

Purling a Stitch

Stockinette Stitch

Joining in a New Color

Knitting Two Stitches Together

Purling Two Stiches Together

Casting Off

MATERIALS

Hat

- 1 × ball each of Rowan Wool/Cotton DK in each of four colors Red (A), Green (B), Claret (C), and Lemon (D)
- Pair each of size 3 (3¼ mm) and size 6 (4 mm) needles

Scarf

- 1 × ball each of Rowan Wool/Cotton DK in each of four colors Red (A), Green (B), Claret (C), and Lemon (D)
- Pair of size 6 (4 mm) needles

MEASUREMENTS

To fit An average child's head

TENSION

22 sts and 30 rows to 4 in. / 10 cm square over st st, using size 6 (4 mm) needles

ABBREVIATIONS

See page 15.

Hat

With size 3 (3¼ mm) needles and A, cast on 105 sts.

Rib row 1 K3, * p3, k3; rep from * to end.

Rib row 2 P3, * k3, p3; rep from * to end.

Rep the last 2 rows 5 more times.

Change to size 6 (4 mm) needles.

Cont in st st and stripes of 4 rows B, 2 rows C, 1 row D, 1 row A, 2 rows B, 2 rows D.

These 12 rows form the stripe sequence.

Work an additional 4 rows.

Shape crown

Row 1 [K11, k2 tog] 8 times, k1.

Row 2 P to end.

Row 3 [K10, k2 tog] 8 times, k1.

Row 4 P to end.

Row 5 [K9, k2 tog] 8 times, k1.

Row 6 P to end.

Row 7 [K8, k2 tog] 8 times, k1.

Row 8 P to end.

Row 9 [K7, k2 tog] 8 times, k1.

Row 10 P to end.

Row 11 [K6, k2 tog] 8 times, k1.

Row 12 P1, [p2 tog, p5] 8 times.

Row 13 [K4, k2 tog] 8 times, k1.

Row 14 P1, [p2 tog, p3] 8 times.

Row 15 [K2, k2 tog] 8 times, k1.

Row 16 P1, [p2 tog, p1] 8 times.

Row 17 [K2 tog] 8 times, k1.

Leaving a long end, cut off yarn and thread through rem sts. Pull up and secure, and remove sts from needle.

MAKE UP

Sew seams together. Weave in yarn ends.

Scarf

With size 6 (4 mm) needles and A, cast on 45 sts.

Rib row 1 K3, * p3, k3; rep from * to end.

Rib row 2 P3, * k3, p3; rep from * to end.

Cont in rib and stripes of 4 rows B, 2 rows C, 1 rows D, 1 row A, 2 rows B, 2 rows D, 10 rows C, 4 rows B, 2 rows C, 1 row D, 1 row A, 2 rows B, 2 rows D, 10 rows A.

These 44 rows form the stripe sequence.

Work an additional 214 rows, ending with 4 rows A, instead of 10 rows.

Cast off in rib.

TO FINISH

Weave in yarn ends.

Striped Glitter Bag

Using different textures and weights of yarn can create a really striking effect. This small handbag is a fantastic example of how colors and textures can work together to produce a really special knitted piece. The color combination is striking yet subtle, with the seed-stitch detail making the colors blend into one another. It is perfect for a first knitting project as there is no shaping involved, and the bag will add a splash of colour to any outfit.

This project uses lots of different types of yarn, including lurex and kid silk, and in places uses more than one strand of yarn at the same time. It is a great project for using up small amounts of left-over yarn.

Techniques Used

Casting On

Knitting a Stitch

Purling a Stitch

Joining in a New Color

Casting Off

MATERIALS

- 1 × 50 g ball each Rowan Cotton Glacé In each of three colors Turquoise (A), Bright Green (B), and Lime Green (C)
- 1 × 50 g ball Rowan Lurex shimmer in Turquoise (D)
- One pair size 8 (5 mm) needles

MEASUREMENTS

Approx 8 in. / 20 cm wide by 5 in. / 13 cm high

ABBREVIATIONS

See page 15.

TENSION

18 stitches and 24 rows to 4 in. / 10 cm square over st st using size 8 (5 mm) needles and Cotton Glacé used double

NOTE

Cotton Glacé is used double throughout and Lurex Shimmer is used triple.

FRONT

With size 8 (5 mm) needles and A, cast on 37.

Cont in patt as folls:

Rows 1 to 6 K in A.

Row 7 K in C.

Row 8 P in B.

Row 9 K in A.

Row 10 P in B.

Row 11 K in D.

Row 12 K in C.

Row 13 K in C.

Row 14 P in C.

Row 15 K in A.

Row 16 P in A.

Row 17 K in C.

Row 18 P in B.

Row 19 K in A.

Row 20 P in B.

Row 21 K in D.

Rows 22 and 23 K in C.

Row 24 K in D.

Row 25 K in C.

Rows 26 to 32 K in A.

Row 31 Using A, k12 sts, cast off center 13 sts, k to end.

Row 32 Using A, k12 sts, turn, cast on 13 sts, turn, k to end.

Rows 33 to 35 K in A.

Cast off.

BACK

With right side facing, using size 8 (5 mm) needles and A, pick up and k37 sts along cast-on edge of back—this counts as row 1.

Rows 2 to 6 K in A.

Row 7 K in B.

Row 8 P in B.

Row 9 K in B.

Row 10 P in B.

Row 11 K in C.

Row 12 P in D.

Row 13 K in C.

Row 14 P in B.

Row 15 K in B.

Row 16 P in C.

Row 17 K in C.

Row 18 P in A.

Row 19 K in A.

Row 20 P in A.

Row 21 K in D.

Row 22 P in D.

Rows 23 to 30 K in A.

Row 31 Using A, k12 sts, cast off center 13 sts, k to end.

Row 32 Using A, k12 sts, turn, cast on 13 sts, turn, k to end.

Rows 33 to 35 K in A.

Cast off.

TO FINISH

Sew side seams together. Weave in yarn ends.

Bobble Hat

One of the most pleasurable things about knitting is choosing yarn and playing with color combinations. I could spend hours laying out yarns on the table and looking at how one color can complement another— sometimes the most unlikely colors make the best companions. Don't be afraid to try inventive color mixes of your own to create your own color palette.

This bobble hat is a fantastic example of color mixing and makes a great accessory for a child's fall wardrobe. Why not get the young ones to make the pom pom? It's so easy, it could be a first step into the exciting world of yarn and knitting.

Techniques Used

Casting On

Knitting a Stitch

Purling a Stitch

Joining in a New Color

Stockinette Stitch

Slipping a Stitch

MATERIALS

- 1 × 50 g ball of Rowan Wool/Cotton DK in each of Bright Red and Dark Red
- Pair each of size 3 (3¼ mm) and size 6 (4 mm) needles

MEASUREMENTS

To fit An average child's head

TENSION

22 sts and 30 rows to 4 in. / 10 cm square over st st using size 6 (4 mm) needles

ABBREVIATIONS

See page 15.

HAT

With size 6 (4 mm) needles and Bright Red, cast on 122 sts.

Rib row 1 K2, * p2, k2; rep from * to end.

Rib row 2 P2, * k2, p2; rep from * to end.

Rep the last 2 rows 9 more times.

Change to size 3 (3¼ mm) needles.

Work an additional 20 rows in rib.

Cut off Bright Red.

Join in Dark Red.

Change to size 6 (4 mm) needles.

Starting with a k row, work 30 rows in st st.

Shape crown

Row 1 K1, [skpo, k10] 10 times, k1.

Row 2 P to end.

Row 3 K1, [skpo, k9] 10 times, k1.

Row 4 P to end.

Row 5 [K1, [skpo, k8] 10 times, k1.

Row 6 P to end.

Row 7 K1, [skpo, k7] 10 times, k1.

Row 8 P to end.

Row 9 K1, [skpo, k6] 10 times, k1.

Row 10 P to end.

Row 11 K1, [skpo, k5] 10 times, k1.

Row 12 P to end.

Row 13 K1, [skpo, k4] 10 times, k1.

Row 14 P to end.

Row 15 K1, [skpo, k3] 10 times, k1.

Row 16 P to end.

Row 17 K1, [skpo, k2] 10 times, k1.

Row 18 P to end.

Row 19 K1, [skpo, k1] 10 times, k1.

Row 20 P to end.

Next row K1, [skpo,] 10 times, k1.

Leaving a long end, cut off yarn and thread through rem sts. Pull up and secure, and remove sts from needle.

TO FINISH

Sew seam together, reversing seam on brim. Using remaining Bright Red, make a pom-pom by winding yarn around two cardboard discs and attach to top of hat. Weave in yarn ends.

Projects *her knits*

Vintage Seed-Stitch Scarf

Inspired by the vintage knitting patterns of the 1940s, the brilliance of this scarf lies in its clever shape and simple styling.

Knitted using a wool 4-ply tweed yarn, the scarf will provide the perfect finishing touch to any outfit, making it an ideal gift for the discerning lady. The scarf is knitted in seed stitch and is a great introduction to simple shaping.

Techniques Used
Casting On
Knitting a Stitch
Purling a Stitch
Seed Stitch
Making a Stitch
Casting Off

MATERIALS

- 2 × 25 g balls of Rowan Yorkshire Tweed 4 ply
- Pair of size 3 (3¼ mm) knitting needles

MEASUREMENTS

Overall length 3½ in. / 80 cm

TENSION

28 sts and 44 rows to 4 in. / 10 cm square over seed st on size 3 (3¼ mm) needles

ABBREVIATIONS

See page 15.

SCARF (make 2 pieces)

With size 3 (3¼ mm) needles cast on 41 sts.

Patt row K2, * p1, k1; rep from * to last 3 sts, p1, k2.

Rep this row to form the seed st pattern with g st border.

Work 1 more row.

Dec row 1 Patt 19 sts, work 3 tog, patt to end.

Work 3 rows.

Dec row 2 Patt 18 sts, work 3 tog, patt to end.

Work 3 rows.

Dec row 3 Patt 17 sts, work 3 tog, patt to end.

Work 3 rows.

Cont in this way, decreasing 2 sts on next and every foll 4th row until 21 sts rem.

Mark end of last row with a colored thread of yarn.

Work 16 rows straight.

Mark end of last row with a colored thread of yarn.

Inc row K2, m1, patt to last 2 sts, m1, k2.

Work 5 rows.

Rep the last 6 rows until there are 61 sts.

Work straight until piece measures 15¾ in. / 40 cm from cast-on edge. Cast off.

Securing ring (worked on one half)

With size 3 (3¼ mm) needles, pick up and k 11 sts between colored threads of yarn.

Work seed st with g st borders for 3½ in. / 9 cm. Cast off.

TO FINISH

Sew cast-off edges together. Sew cast-off edge of securing ring to back of picked up sts, enclosing scarf. Thread other end of scarf through ring. Weave in yarn ends.

Sky-Blue Poncho and Beret

The beret can to be worn in various ways, either pulled down around the ears or worn to the side. It is knitted in a rich mohair mix yarn and is ideal for keeping warm on a cold day, while making a great fashion statement.

The matching poncho is knitted in single rib, making it a dense and practical fabric. It is very simple to put together and can be worn in a variety of ways—experiment to see how it looks best on you.

Techniques Used

Casting On

Knitting a Stitch

Purling a Stitch

Making a Stitch

Knitting Two Stitches Together

Casting Off

MATERIALS

Poncho

- 7 × 50 g balls Rowan Kid Classic
- Pair of size 8 (5 mm) needles

Beret

- 1 × 50 g ball Rowan Kid Classic
- Pair each of size 6 (4 mm) and size 8 (5 mm) needles

MEASUREMENTS

One size to fit 12 years to adult

TENSION

20 sts and 25 rows to 4 in. / 10 cm square over rib using size 8 (5 mm) needles

ABBREVIATIONS

See page 15.

Poncho

With size 8 (5 mm) needles cast on 140 sts.

Rib row * K1, p1; rep from * to end.

This row forms the rib.

Cont in rib until piece measures 55 in. / 140 cm from cast-on edge.

Cast off in rib.

TO FINISH

Fold the piece in half widthwise and sew a seam 10¾ in. / 27 cm long, starting at cast-on and cast-off edges, along row ends.

Cut remaining yarn into 18 in. / 46 cm lengths and knot 6 together to form fringe along cast-on and cast-off edges.

Beret

With size 6 (4 mm) needles, cast on 84 sts.

Rib row * K1, p1; rep from * to end.

Rep this row 15 times, inc 1 st at center of last row. 85 sts.

Inc row [K3, m1] 28 times, k1. 113 sts.

Change to size 8 (5 mm) needles.

Starting with a p row, cont in st st.

Work 9 rows.

Inc row [K8, m1] 14 times, k1. 127 sts.

Work 9 rows.

Shape top

Dec row [K7, k2 tog] 14 times, k1. 113 sts.

Work 3 rows.

Dec row [K13, k3 tog] 7 times, k1. 99 sts.

Work 3 rows.

Dec row [K11, k3 tog] 7 times, k1. 85 sts.

Work 3 rows.

Dec row [K9, k3 tog] 7 times, k1. 71 sts.

Work 3 rows.

Dec row [K7, k3 tog] 7 times, k1. 57 sts.

Work 1 row.

Dec row [K5, k3 tog] 7 times, k1. 43 sts.

Dec row [P3, p3 tog] 7 times, k1. 29 sts.

Dec row [K1, k3 tog] 7 times, k1. 15 sts.

TO FINISH

Break off yarn thread through rem sts, pull up, and secure. Remove sts from needle. Sew seam up. Weave in yarn ends.

Striped Tote Bag

This is another relatively easy color work project; perfect for beginner knitters looking to try out Intarsia knitting.

Knitted in 100 per cent cotton, this bag will be durable and practical, as well as the ultimate in style.

The bag has a knitted hem and could be lined with fabric, if you wish, to give it extra stability.

Techniques Used

Casting On

Stockinette Stitch

Intarsia Color Work

Joining in a New Color

Casting Off

MATERIALS

- 1 × 50 g ball of Rowan Handknit Cotton in each of four colors, Beige (A), Light Brown (B), Cream (C), and Sea Green (D)
- Pair each size 5 (3¾ mm) and size 6 (4 mm) needles
- Two size 6 (4 mm) double-pointed needles
- 1 magnetic bag closure (optional)
- Lining fabric (optional)
- Firm cardboard

MEASUREMENTS

Approx. 12½ in. / 32 cm wide by 10½ in. / 27 cm long

TENSION

20 sts and 28 rows to 4 in. / 10 cm square over st st using size 6 (4 mm) needles

ABBREVIATIONS

See page 15.

NOTE

To do Intarsia knitting, see page 50.

Tote Bag

BACK

With size 6 (4 mm) needles and B, cast on 64 sts.

Beg with a k row work in st st as follows:

Work 9 rows.

Row 10 (hemline) K to end.

Cont in st st.

Row 11 Knit.

Row 12 Purl.

Join in yarn A but do not break off yarn B.

Note: When working single-row stripes, to avoid unnecessary ends, work using a pair of double-pointed needles as follows:

Row 13 K in A, slip stitches back to the other end of needle.

Row 14 K in B.

Row 15 P in A, slip stitches back to the other end of needle.

Row 16 Purl in B.

Continue to knit, slide, knit, and purl, slide, purl using color sequence as follows:

Row 17 K in D.

Row 18 K in B.

Row 19 P in A.

Row 20 P in C.

Row 21 K in B.

Row 22 K in A.

Change back to size 6 (4 mm) needles.

Using st st and intarsia technique work as follows:

Row 23 K 5A, [2D, 8C, 8B, 8A] twice, 2D, 5C.

Row 24 P 5C, [2D, 8A, 8B, 8C] twice, 2D, 5A.

Rows 25 to 80 Rep rows 23 and 24, 28 times.

Cont in st st and stripe patt as follows:

Rows 81 to 92 Work 2 rows B, 2 rows A, 2 rows C, 2 rows A, 2 rows B, 2 rows D.

Cont in B only.

Work 4 rows.

Cast off 6 sts at the beginning of the next 2 rows.

BASE

Work 10 rows in B.

FRONT

Cast on 6 sts at the beginning of the next 2 rows.

Work 4 rows in B.

To complete bag, reading k for p and p for k and working intarsia stripes in same order as on back, work backward from row 92 to 1.

Cast off.

STRAPS (MAKE TWO)

With size 5 (3¾ mm) needles and A, cast on 54 sts.

Beg with k row, work 15 rows st st.

Cast off.

TO FINISH

Lay work flat and use as guide for cutting out lining fabric, adding seam allowance of ⅝ in. / 1½ cm.

Sew side seams together.

Sew across bottom gusset seams.

Fold down hem at top, and slip stitch in place.

Fold straps in half lengthwise on rs and slip stitch cast-on and cast-off edges together.

Position handles and stitch in place. Weave in yarn ends.

TO LINE BAG

Stitch side seams of lining together on ws, then bottom gusset seam. Fold over top edge of lining and press to ws.

Slide lining into bag and slip stitch in place around upper edge, just above knitted hemline.

Cut firm cardboard to size of bag base. Use as a guide for cutting out 2 base linings, adding seam allowance.

With right sides together, sew base lining on 3 sides. Turn to rs and fold raw edges to ws and press. Slip cardboard inside. Slip stitch folded edges together.

Place covered cardboard into base of bag.

Sew on magnetic bag closure in center of upper hem between handles, if desired.

Sweater with Beaded Edging

This lovely beaded sweater is bound to be a favorite, with its subtle color combination and sophisticated design. Knitted in a wool-tweed yarn, this garment has a slightly fitted shape to flatter your figure, with beads at the cuff and welt edges, and on the neckline. The seed-stitch detail featured alongside the beads adds a beautiful finishing touch.

Beading is very easy but be sure to thread sufficient beads onto the yarn before you start knitting, as breaks in the yarn can later be apparent on the right side of the work.

Techniques Used

- Casting On
- Knitting a Stitch
- Purling a Stitch
- Beading
- Stockinette Stitch
- Slipping a Stitch
- Knitting Two Stitches Together
- Making a Stitch
- Casting Off
- Purling Two Stitches Together

MATERIALS

- 7 (8:8:9) × 50 g balls of Rowan Yorkshire Tweed DK
- Pair size 6 (4 mm) needles
- Circular size 6 (4 mm) knitting needle
- 625 (658:691:730) beads

MEASUREMENTS

To fit bust			
34	36	38	40 in.
86	92	97	102 cm

Sweater Measurements

Bust

39	41¼	43½	46¾ in.
99	105	111	119 cm

Length to shoulder

19¾	20	20½	21 in.
50	51	52	53 cm

Sleeve length

17	17	17½	17½ in.
43	43	44	44 cm

TENSION

20 sts and 28 rows to 4 in. / 10 cm square over st st using size 6 (4 mm) needles

ABBREVIATIONS

B1 yarn to front, slip next st, push bead up close to work, yarn to back.

Also see page 15.

BACK

Thread 149 (158:167:179) beads onto yarn.

With size 6 (4 mm) needles and M, cast on 101 (107:113:121) sts.

Row 1 (ws) K1, * p1, k1; rep from * to end.

Row 2 K1, * B1, k1; rep from * to end.

Row 3 P to end.

Row 4 K2, * B1, k1; rep from * to last 3 sts, B1, k2.

Row 5 P to end.

Row 6 K1, * B1, k1; rep from * to end.

Row 7 K1, * p1, k1; rep from * to end.

Beg with a k row, cont in st st, as follows:

Work 8 rows.

Row 9 K5 (6:7:8), skpo, k25 (26:27:28), k2 tog, k33 (35:37:41), skpo, k25 (26:27:28), k2 tog, k5 (6:7:8).

Work 5 rows.

Row 15 K5 (6:7:8), skpo, k23 (24:25:26), k2 tog, k33 (35:37:41), skpo, k23 (24:25:26), k2 tog, k5 (6:7:8).

Work 5 rows.

Row 21 K5 (6:7:8), skpo, k21 (22:23:24), k2 tog, k33 (35:37:41), skpo, k21 (22:23:24), k2 tog, k5 (6:7:8).

Work 5 rows.

Row 27 K5 (6:7:8), skpo, k19 (20:21:22), k2 tog, k33 (35:37:41), skpo, k19 (20:21:22), k2 tog, k5 (6:7:8).

Work 5 rows.

Row 33 K5 (6:7:8), skpo, k17 (18:19:20), k2 tog, k33 (35:37:41), skpo, k17 (18:19:20), k2 tog, k5 (6:7:8). 81 (87:93:101) sts.

Cont straight until back measures 6¼ in. / 16 cm from cast-on edge, ending with a p row.

Next row K5 (6:7:8), m1, k to last 5 (6:7:8) sts, m1, k5 (6:7:8).

Work 3 rows.

Rep the last 4 rows until there are 101 (107:113:121) sts.

Cont straight until back measures 11¾ (11¾:12¼:12¼) in. / 30 (30:31:31) cm from cast-on edge, ending with a p row.

Shape armholes

Cast off 5 (5:6:6) sts at beg of next 2 rows.

Dec 1 st at each end of next and every foll alt row until 81 (85:87:91) sts rem. **

Cont in st st until back measures 19¾ (20:20½:21) in. / 50 (51:52:53) cm from cast-on edge, ending with a p row.

Shape shoulders

Cast off 11 (12:12:12) sts at beg of next 2 rows and 12 (12:12:13) sts at beg of foll 2 rows.

Cast off rem 35 (37:39:41) sts.

FRONT

Work as given for back to **.

P 1 row.

Shape neck

Next row K37 (39:40:42) sts, turn and work on these sts only for first side of neck shaping.

P 1 row.

Next row K to last 4 st, k2tog, k2.

Next row P to end.

Next row K to end.

Next row P2, p2 tog, p to end.

Next row K to end.

Next row P to end.

Rep the last 6 rows until 23 (24:24:25) sts rem.

Work straight until front measures same as back to shoulder shaping, ending at armhole edge.

Shape shoulder

Cast off 11 (12:12:12) sts at beg of next row.

Work 1 row.

Cast off rem 12 (12:12:13) sts.

Rejoin yarn to rem sts, cast off 7 sts, k to end.

P 1 row.

Next row K2, skpo, k to end.

Next row P to end.

Next row K to end.

Next row P to last 4 sts, p2tog tbl, p2.

Next row K to end.

Next row P to end.

Rep the last 6 rows until 23 (24:24:25) sts rem.

Work straight until front measures same as back to shoulder shaping, ending at armhole edge.

Shape shoulder

Cast off 11 (12:12:12) sts at beg of next row.

Work 1 row.

Cast off rem 12 (12:12:13) sts.

SLEEVES

Thread 56 (62:68:74) beads onto yarn.

With size 6 (4 mm) needles and M cast on 39 (43:47:51) sts.

Row 1 (ws) K1, * p1, k1; rep from * to end.

Row 2 K1, * B1, k1; rep from * to end.

Row 3 P to end.

Row 4 K2, * B1, k1; rep from * to last 3 sts, B1, k2.

Row 5 P to end.

Row 6 K1, * B1, k1; rep from * to end.

Row 7 K1, * p1, k1; rep from * to end.

Beg with a k row, cont in st st, as follows:

Work 2 rows.

Inc row K3, m1, k to last 3 sts, m1, k3.

Work 5 rows.

Rep the last 6 rows until there are 75 (79:83:87) sts.

Cont straight until sleeve measures 17 (17:17½:17½) in. / 43 (43:44:44) cm from cast-on edge, ending with a p row.

Shape sleeve top

Cast off 5 (5:6:6) sts at beg of next 2 rows.

Dec 1 st at each end of next 4 rows, then 3 foll alt rows, then every foll 4th row until 37 (39:41:43) sts rem. Then on every foll alt row until 27 sts rem.

Cast off 3 sts at beg of next 2 rows.

Cast off.

COLLAR

Sew shoulder seams together.

With size 6 (4 mm) circular needle and rs facing, pick up and k55 sts up rs of front neck shaping, k across 35 (37:39:41) sts across back neck, pick up and k55 sts down left side of front neck. 145 (147:149:151) sts.

Cont in seed st.

Rows 1 and 2 Seed st to last 50 sts, turn.

Rows 3 and 4 Seed st to last 40 sts, turn.

Rows 5 and 6 Seed st to last 30 sts, turn.

Rows 7 and 8 Seed st to last 20 sts, turn.

Rows 9 and 10 Seed st to last 10 sts, turn.

Row 11 Seed st to end.

Break off yarn.

Thread 215 (218:221:224) beads onto yarn.

Row 12 K1, * B1, k1; rep from * to end.

Row 13 P to end.

Row 14 K2, * B1, k1; rep from * to last 3 sts, B1, k2.

Row 15 P to end.

Row 16 K1, * B1, k1; rep from * to end.

Cast off in purl.

TO FINISH

Sew sleeves in position. Sew side and sleeve seams together. Sew row ends of collar to cast off sts at center front. Weave in yarn ends.

Pastel Beaded Cardigan

This cardigan provides a good introduction to the Fair Isle technique—it has a gap of only three stitches between a color change, with no more than two colors to a row.

The beaded edge gives this cardigan a touch of sparkle and adds weight to the cast-on edge. The combination of light colors, and a few rows of bead knitting worked among the Fair Isle give the cardigan a smart feminine feel.

Techniques Used

Casting On
Stockinette Stitch
Fair Isle Color Work
Beading
Casting Off
Knitting Two Stitches Together

MATERIALS

- 12 (13:14) × 50 g balls of Rowan Glacé Cotton in Lilac (M)
- 1 × 50 g ball in each of 4 colors Purple, Pink, Aqua, and Green
- Pair each of size 2 (2¾ mm) and size 3 (3¼ mm) needles
- 500 (550:600) beads
- 9 buttons

TENSION

23 sts and 32 rows to 4 in. / 10 cm square over st st using size 3 (3¼ mm) needles

ABBREVIATIONS

See page 15.

MEASUREMENTS

To fit bust		
34	36	38 in.
86	92	97 cm

Cardigan Measurements		
Bust		
36½	39¼	41¾ in.
93	100	106 cm
Length to shoulder		
20	21	21½ in.
51	53	55 cm
Sleeve length		
16	16½	17 in.
41	42	43 cm

NOTE

When working in patt from chart (see page 109), odd-numbered rows are k rows and are read from right to left. Even-number rows are p rows and are read from left to right. Strand yarn not in use loosely across ws of work.

When placing a bead, take yarn to rs of work, slide bead up close to work, slip next st pwise, take yarn to back of work.

To work Fair Isle, see pages 52–59.

BACK

Thread 162 (174:186) beads onto a ball of yarn in main color.

With size 2 (2¾ mm) needles and M, using thumb method (see page 20), cast on 109 (117:125) sts, placing a bead between each st.

P 5 rows.

Change to size 3 (3¼ mm) needles.

Beg with a p row, cont in st st.

Work 3 rows.

Work in patt from chart (see page 109).

Row 1 Work across 4-st patt rep from chart, 27 (29:31) times, then work edge st.

Row 2 Work edge st from chart, then work across 4-st patt rep from chart 27 (29:31) times.

These 2 rows form patt. Cont to end of chart.

Now work straight until back measures 11 (11½:12) in. / 28 (29:30) cm from cast-on edge, ending with a ws row.

Shape armholes

Cast off 4 sts at beg of next 2 rows.

Dec 1 st at each end of next 7 (9:11) rows and 7 foll alt rows. 73 (77:81) sts rem.

Cont in st st until back measures 19¼ (20:21) in. / 49 (51:53) cm from cast-on edge, ending with a ws row.

Shape back neck and shoulders

Cast off 6 sts at beg of next 2 rows.

Next row Cast off 6, k next 10 (11:12) sts, turn and work on these sts for first side of neck shaping.

Next row Cast off 4 sts, p to end.

Next row Cast off rem 7 (8:9) sts.

With rs facing, rejoin yarn to rem sts, cast off 27 (29:31) sts, k to end.

Complete to match first side.

LEFT FRONT

Thread 78 (84:90) beads onto a ball of yarn in main color.

With size 2 (2¾ mm) needles and M, using thumb method, cast on 53 (57:61) sts, placing a bead between each st.

P 5 rows.

Change to size 3 (3¼ mm) needles.

Beg with a p row, cont in st st.

Work 3 rows.

Work in patt from chart.

Row 1 Work across 4-st patt rep from chart, 13 (14:15) times, then work edge st.

Row 2 Work edge st, then work across 4-st patt rep from chart 13 (14:15) times.

These 2 rows form patt. Cont to end of chart.

Using M, cont until front measures 11 (11½:12) in. / 28 (29:30) cm from cast-on edge, ending with a ws row.

Shape armhole

Cast off 4 sts at beg of next row.

P 1 row.

Dec 1 st at armhole edge of next 7 (9:11) rows and 7 foll alt rows. 35 (37:39) sts rem.

Cont in st st until front measures 16½ (17¼:18) in. / 42 (44:46) cm from cast-on edge, ending with a ws row.

Shape front neck

Next row K to last 8 (9:10) sts, turn, and leave rem sts on a stitch holder.

P 1 row.

Dec 1 st at neck edge on next 6 rows and foll 2 alt rows. 19 (20:21) sts.

Work straight until front matches back to shoulder shaping, ending at armhole edge.

Shape shoulder

Cast off 6 sts at beg of next and foll alt row.

P 1 row.

Next row Cast off rem 7 (8:9) sts.

RIGHT FRONT

Thread 78 (84:90) beads onto a ball of yarn in main color.

With size 2 (2¾ mm) needles and thumb method, cast on 53 (57:61) sts, placing a bead between each st.

P 5 rows.

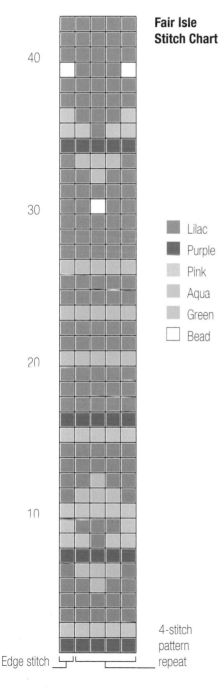

Fair Isle Stitch Chart

40

30

- Lilac
- Purple
- Pink
- Aqua
- Green
- Bead

20

10

4-stitch pattern repeat

Edge stitch

Change to size 3 (3¼ mm) needles.

Beg with a p row, cont in st st.

Work 3 rows.

Work in patt from chart.

Row 1 Work across 4-st patt rep from chart 13 (14:15) times, then work edge st.

Row 2 Work edge st, then work across 4-st patt rep from chart 13 (14:15) times.

These 2 rows form patt. Cont to end of chart.

Now work straight until front measures 11 (11½:12) in. / 28 (29:30) cm from cast-on edge, ending with a rs row.

Shape armhole

Cast off 4 sts at beg of next row.

Dec 1 st at armhole edge of next 7 (9:11) rows and 7 foll alt rows. 35 (37:39) sts rem.

Cont in st st until front measures 16½ (17¼:18) in. / 42 (44:46) cm from cast-on edge, ending with a ws row.

Shape front neck

Next row K8 (9:10) sts, leave these sts on a stitch holder, k to end.

P 1 row.

Dec 1 st at neck edge on next 6 rows and foll 2 alt rows. 19 (20:21) sts.

Work straight until front matches back to shoulder shaping, ending at armhole edge.

Work 1 row.

Dec 1 st at each end of next and 4 (5:6) foll alt rows.

Dec 1 st at each end of next 2 rows.

Cast off 4 sts at beg of next 2 rows.

Cast off rem 21 (23:25) sts.

NECK BORDER

Sew shoulder seams together.

With rs facing, with size 2 (2¾ mm) needles and M, slip 8 (9:10) sts from holder onto needle. Pick up and k24 sts up rs of front neck, 37 (39:41) sts from back neck, 24 sts down left front neck, k8 (9:10) sts from front neck holder. 101 (105:109) sts.

K4 rows.

Cast off.

BUTTONHOLE BAND

With size 2 (2¾ mm) needles and rs facing, and using M, pick up and k93 (102:111) sts along right front edge to beg of neck shaping.

K 1 row.

Buttonhole row (K8 [9:10], k2 tog, yf) 9 times, k3.

K 2 rows.

Cast off.

BUTTON BAND

With size 2 (2¾ mm) needles and rs facing and using M, starting at neck shaping, pick up and k93 (102:111) sts along left front edge.

K 4 rows.

Cast off.

TO FINISH

Sew side seams together. Join sleeve seams. Sew in sleeves. Sew on 9 buttons, placing a bead in center of button and passing needle through bead and button when sewing on. Weave in yarn ends.

Shape shoulder

Cast off 6 sts at beg of next and foll alt row.

P 1 row.

Next row Cast off rem 7 (8:9) sts.

SLEEVES

Thread 52 (56:60) beads onto a ball of yarn in main color.

With size 2 (2¾ mm) needles and M, using thumb method (see page 20), cast on 53 (57:61) sts, placing a bead between each st.

P 5 rows.

Change to size 3 (3¼ mm) needles.

Beg with a p row, cont in st st.

Work 3 rows.

K 1 row Purple.

P 1 row Pink.

Cont in M only.

Inc 1 st at each end of the 3rd and every foll 8th row until there are 79 (83:87) sts.

Cont straight until sleeve measures 16 (16½:17) in. / 41 (42:43) cm from cast-on edge, ending with a p row.

Shape sleeve top

Cast off 4 sts at beg of next 2 rows.

Dec 1 st at each end of the next 5 rows and 5 foll alt rows. 51 (55:59) sts.

Now dec 1 st at each end of every foll 4th row until 43 (47:51) sts rem.

Lacework Fitted Cap

Knitting as a hobby is no longer a money-saving and economical necessity and it can be more expensive to buy yarn to complete a project than to purchase a mass-produced knitted garment.

You will be pleased to hear that this project takes just one ball of yarn, which is great if you want to complete a small project before launching into one that requires a lot of time, yarn, and substantial expense.

Knitted in a very simple lace pattern this lovely hat can also be completed quickly, making it a perfect starting point for any new knitter.

Techniques Used

Casting On

Knitting a Stitch

Knitting Two Stitches Together

Slipping a Stitch

MATERIALS

- 1× 50 g ball of Rowan Calmer
- Pair of size 6 (4 mm) needles
- One size 10 (6 mm) needle

MEASUREMENTS

To fit: average head

TENSION

21 sts and 28 rows to 4 in. / 10 cm square over patt using size 6 (4 mm) needles and size 10 (6 mm) needle

ABBREVIATIONS

See page 15.

HAT

With size 6 (4 mm) needles, cast on 91 sts.

K5 rows.

Now work in patt, as follows:

Row 1 With size 10 (6 mm) needle, k1, * yf, k2 tog; rep from * to end.

Rows 2, 3, and 4 With size 6 (4 mm) needles, k to end.

These 4 rows form the patt and are rep throughout.

Cont in patt until cap measures 6¼ in. / 16 cm from cast-on edge, ending with row 2.

Shape crown

Dec row 1 K1, [skpo, k3] 18 times. 73 sts.

Work 3 rows.

Dec row 2 K1, [skpo, k2] 18 times. 55 sts.

Work 3 rows.

Dec row 3 K1, [skpo, k1] 18 times. 37 sts.

Work 3 rows.

Dec row 4 K1, [skpo] 18 times. 19 sts.

Work 3 rows.

Dec row 4 K1, [skpo] 9 times. 10 sts.

Leaving a long end, cut off yarn and thread through rem sts. Pull up and secure.

TO FINISH

Join seam. Weave in yarn ends.

Seed-Stitch Beret and Scarf

Consistently fashionable and extremely practical, this beret is a must for any wardrobe. The matching scarf completes the look. Worn together the two pieces will create a striking effect.

The set is a great exercise for new knitters, introducing them to the process of simple shaping. Stitches are decreased at one end and increased at the other end of every alternate row to create the scarf's pointed edges.

Techniques Used

Casting On

Knitting a Stitch

Purling a Stitch

Seed Stitch

Making a Stitch

Casting Off

MATERIALS

Beret

- 1 × 50 g ball of Rowan Yorkshire Tweed DK
- Pair each size 5 (3¾ mm) and size 6 (4 mm) needles

Scarf

- One 50 g ball of Rowan Yorkshire Tweed DK
- Pair size 6 (4 mm) needles

MEASUREMENTS

Beret: to fit average head; Scarf: 3 in. / 8 cm wide by 35 in. / 89 cm long.

TENSION

20 sts and 36 rows to 4 in. / 10 cm square over seed st using size 6 (4 mm) needles

ABBREVIATIONS

See page 15.

Beret

With size 5 (3¾ mm) needles, cast on 102 sts.

Rib row * K1, p1; rep from * to end.

Rep the last row 6 times more.

Inc row K1, * m1, k3; rep from * to last 2 sts, m1, k2. 136 sts.

Change to size 6 (4 mm) needles.

Seed st row 1 * K1, p1; rep from * to end.

Seed st row 2 * P1, k1; rep from * to end.

These 2 rows form the seed st.

Cont in seed st until work measures 4 in. / 10 cm from cast-on edge.

Shape top

Dec row K1, * work 3 tog, seed st 24; rep from * to end.

Seed st 1 row.

Dec row K1, * work 3 tog, seed st 22; rep from * to end.

Seed st 1 row.

Dec row K1, * work 3 tog, seed st 20; rep from * to end.

Seed st 1 row.

Cont in this way decreasing 10 sts on every alt row until 16 sts rem.

Seed st 1 row.

Break off yarn thread through rem sts, pull up, and secure.

TO FINISH

Sew up seam.

Scarf

With size 6 (4 mm) needles, cast on 20 sts.

Seed st row 1(rs) * K1, p1; rep from * to end.

Seed st row 2 * P1, k1; rep from * to end.

These 2 rows form the seed st patt.

Next row Inc in first st, seed st to last 2 sts, work 2 tog.

Next row Seed st to end.

Rep the last 2 rows until scarf measures 6¼ in. / 16 cm from cast-on edge, ending with a ws row.

Divide for slit

Next row Inc in first st, seed st 7, work 2 tog, turn, and work on these 10 sts.

Next row Seed st to end.

Next row Inc in first st, seed st to last 2 sts, work 2 tog.

Rep the last 2 rows 9 times more.

Break off yarn and leave sts on a spare needle.

Rejoin yarn to rem sts.

Next row Inc in first st, seed st 7, work 2 tog.

Next row Seed st to end.

Rep the last 2 rows 9 times more and the first row once more.

Next row Seed st to end, then seed st across sts on spare needle. 20 sts.

Cont in patt until scarf measures 35 in. / 89 cm.

Cast off in seed st. Weave in yarn ends.

Felted Purse

This bag is first knitted as two rectangles, then sewn together and popped into the washing machine at a low temperature to create the felted effect. The leather thong, used as a design detail gives the finished purse a sophisticated, elegant look.

If the water is too hot, your knitted piece will be ruined, so it is always a good idea to try a test piece of knitting in your washing machine first. If you are felting by hand, rub the piece vigorously in hot water and soap flakes, then immerse it straight into cold water. Repeat a couple of times and the piece will felt.

Techniques Used

Casting On

Stockinette Stitch

Casting Off

MATERIALS

- 2 × 50 g balls Rowan Yorkshire Tweed DK
- One pair each size 3 (3¼ mm) and size 6 (4 mm) needles
- 3¼ yd / 2 m leather thong
- 1 magnetic bag closure
- Lining fabric, approx. 13 in. wide × 20 in. high
- Large-eyed, blunt-tipped needle

MEASUREMENTS

Approx. 9½ in. / 24 cm wide by 8¼ in. / 21 cm high

Measurements are approximate as felting is not an exact science.

TENSION

20 sts and 28 rows to 4 in. / 10 cm square over st st using size 6 (4 mm) needles

Note: Using the recommended size needle will result in a firm felted fabric. For a softer fabric, use a larger-needle size.

ABBREVIATIONS

See page 15.

BACK

With size 6 (4 mm) needles, cast on 50 sts.

Beg with a k row, cont in st st for 12 in. / 30 cm, ending with a p row.

Cast off.

FRONT

With rs facing, using size 6 (4 mm) needles, pick up and k 50 sts along cast-on edge of back.

Beg with a p row, work in st st for 12 in. / 30 cm, ending with a p row.

Cast off.

Carefully weave in yarn ends.

HANDLES (Make 2)

With size 3 (3¼ mm) needles cast on 75 sts.

K 6 rows.

Cast off.

Carefully weave in yarn ends.

FELTING

Note: Several factors determine the finished felted look. It is advisable to gradually felt your work by washing twice in medium-hot water, rather than washing once in very hot water, which can result in a cardboard-like texture. Avoid washing a knitted piece with other items in the machine at the same time which causes an abrasive action and results in a harder texture.

Place all knitted pieces in the washing machine and wash at 120–140° F / 50–60° C.

Pull the felted piece to the correct size and shape, and dry. Repeat the washing process until the desired felted look is achieved. Tumble drying will continue to shrink and felt the work.

TO FINISH

Lay work flat and use as a guide for cutting out lining fabric, adding seam allowances of ⅝ in. / 1½ cm all around.

Join side seams.

Fold over 1½ in. / 4 cm at upper edge to ws to form hem. Slip stitch into place.

Position handles and stitch into place.

Cut leather thong in half. Thread one half into a large-eyed blunt-tipped needle.

Starting from the center front of bag and using the knit stitches as a guide to stay straight, stitch large running stitches around the bag, meeting back again at center front.

Repeat with the second half of the thong, going in and out the same holes. Tie ends together at center front in a knot.

TO LINE PURSE

With right sides together, stitch the sides and base of the two lining fabric rectangles.

Slide lining into bag, fold over top edge to ws, and slip stitch in place around upper edge just above knitted hemline.

Sew on magnetic bag closure in center of hem between handles.

Fitted Turtleneck Sweater

This super-soft sweater is a classic garment—it can be dressed up or down to great effect.

It is knitted with two yarns together. You do not need to twist the yarns in any way; just start knitting with both yarns simultaneously and you will find that you are rewarded with a lovely tweedlike knitted fabric.

Why not try different color combinations? You may be surprised at which colors work well together.

Techniques Used

Casting On

Knitting a Stitch

Purling a Stitch

Stockinette Stitch

Slipping a Stitch

Knitting Two Stitches Together

Casting Off

Making a Stitch

MATERIALS

- 10 (11:11:12:12:13) × 25 g balls of Rowan Yorkshire Tweed 4 ply
- 5 (6:6:6:6:7) × 25 g balls of Rowan Kidsilk Haze
- Pair each size 3 (3¼ mm) and size 6 (4 mm) needles

TENSION

23 sts and 30 rows to 4 in. / 10 cm square over st st using size 6 (4 mm) needles, using 1 strand each of Yorkshire Tweed 4-ply and Kidsilk Haze held together

ABBREVIATIONS

See page 15.

MEASUREMENTS

To fit bust					
32	34	36	38	40	42 in.
81	86	92	97	102	107 cm

Sweater measurements					
Bust					
35	37	39	41	43	45 in.
89	94	99	104	109	114 cm
Length to shoulder					
22	22	22½	22½	223	23 in.
56	56	57	57	58	58 cm
Sleeve length					
17	17	17¼	17¼	17¾	17¾ in.
43	43	44	44	45	45 cm

NOTE

Use one strand each of Yorkshire tweed 4 ply and Kidsilk haze together throughout.

BACK

With size 3 (3¼ mm) needles, cast on 102 (110:114:122:126:134) sts.

Row 1 K2, * p2, k2; rep from * to end.

Row 2 P2, * k2, p2; rep from * to end.

Rep the last 2 rows once more, increasing 2 sts evenly across last row on **1st, 3rd, and 5th sizes only.** 104 (110:116:122:128:134) sts.

Change to size 6 (4 mm) needles.

Beg with a k row, cont in st st, as follows:

Work 8 rows.

Dec row K6, skpo, k to last 8 sts, k2 tog, k6.

Work 5 rows.

Rep the last 6 rows 5 times more and the dec row again. 90 (96:102:108:114:120) sts.

Cont straight until back measures 8 in. / 20 cm from cast-on edge, ending with a ws row.

Inc row K3, m1, k to last 3 sts, m1, k3.

Work 5 rows.

Rep the last 6 rows five times more and the inc row again. 104 (110:116:122:128:134) sts.

Cont straight until back measures 13½ (13½:13¾:13¾:14¼:14¼) in. / 34 (34:35:35:36:36) cm from cast-on edge, ending with a ws row.

Shape armholes

Cast off 5 (5:6:6:7:7) sts at beg of next 2 rows.

Dec 1 st at each end of next and every foll alt row until 80 (84:86:88:92:96) sts rem.

Cont in st st until back measures 21¼ (21½:22:22½:22¾:23¼) in. / 54 (55:56:57:58:59) cm from cast-on edge, ending with a ws row.

Shape neck

Next row K20 (21:22:23:24:25) sts, turn and work on these sts for first side of neck shaping.

Dec 1 st at neck edge on next 4 rows. 16 (17:18:19:20:21) sts.

Work 1 row.

Shape shoulder

Cast off 8 (8:9:9:10:10) sts at beg of next row.

Work 1 row.

Cast off rem 8 (9:9:10:10:11) sts.

With rs facing, slip center 40 (42:42:42:44:46) sts onto a holder, rejoin yarn to rem sts, k to end.

Complete to match first side of neck shaping.

FRONT

Work as given for back until front measures 20 (20½:21:21¼:21½:22) in. / 51 (52:53:54:55:56) cm from cast-on edge, ending with a ws row.

Shape neck

Next row K25 (26:27:28:29:30) sts, turn and work on these sts for first side of neck shaping.

Dec 1 st at neck edge on next 9 rows. 16 (17:18:19:20:21) sts.

Shape shoulder

Cast off 8 (8:9:9:10:10) sts at beg of next row.

Work 1 row.

Cast off rem 8 (9:9:10:10:11) sts.

With rs facing, slip center 30 (32:32:32:34:36) sts onto a holder, rejoin yarn to rem sts, K to end.

Complete to match first side of neck shaping.

SLEEVES

With size 3 (3¼ mm) needles cast on 42 (46:50:54:58:62) sts.

Work 8 rows rib as given for back on page 116.

Change to size 6 (4 mm) needles.

Beg with a k row, cont in st st.

Work 4 rows.

Inc row K3, m1, k to last 3 sts, m1, k3.

Work 5 rows.

Rep the last 6 rows until there are 78 (82:86:90:94:98) sts.

Cont straight until sleeve measures 17 (17:17¼:17¼:17¾:17¾) in. / 43 (43:44:44:45:45:) cm from cast-on edge, ending with a p row.

Shape sleeve top

Cast off 5 (5:6:6:7:7) sts at beg of next 2 rows.

Dec 1 st at each end of the next 4 rows then 3 foll alt rows then every foll 4th row until 40 (42:44:46:48:50) sts rem; then on every foll alt row until 28 sts rem.

Cast off 3 sts at beg of next 2 rows.

Cast off rem sts.

COLLAR

Join right shoulder.

With rs facing and size 3 (3¼ mm) needles, pick up and k13 sts down left side of front neck, k across 30 (32:32:32:34:36) sts from front holder, pick up and k13 sts up rs of front neck, 11 sts down rs of back neck, k across 40 (42:42:42:44:46) sts from back neck holder, pick up and k11 sts up left side of front neck. 118 (122:122:122:126:130) sts.

Row 1 P2, * k2, p2; rep from * to end.

Row 2 K2, * p2, k2; rep from * to end.

Rep the last 2 rows until collar measures 3¼ in. / 8 cm.

Change to size 6 (4 mm) needles.

Cont in rib for an additional 3½ in. / 9 cm.

Cast off in rib.

TO FINISH

Join left shoulder and collar seam, reversing seam on collar. Sew on sleeves. Join side and sleeve seams. Weave in yarn ends.

Woman's Ribbed Scarf

This scarf is knitted using the broken rib stitch. This means that you only work in rib every alternate row and break the rib sequence with purl stitches on every wrong side row. It is a great rib stitch if you have difficulty keeping your knitted gauge even.

Knitted in a chunky wool yarn, this scarf is quick and easy and a great project for knitters who have mastered knit and purl stitches and want to use them together in the same row. Don't forget to take the yarn between the needles and to the back of the work before working a knit stitch, and bring it to the front between the needles before working a purl stitch.

Techniques Used

Casting On

Knitting a Stitch

Purling a Stitch

Casting Off

MATERIALS

- 3 × balls of Rowan Chunky Print
- Pair of size 11 (8 mm) needles

MEASUREMENTS

Approx. 6¼ in. / 16 cm wide by 56 in. / 142 cm long

TENSION

18 sts and 20 rows to 4 in. / 10 cm square over rib patt using size 11 (8 mm) needles

ABBREVIATIONS

See page 15.

SCARF

With size 11 (8 mm) needles, cast on 29 sts.

Rib row 1 * P2, k2; rep from * to last st, p1.

Rib row 2 K2, * p2, k2; rep from * to last 3 sts, p2, k1.

These 2 rows form the patt and are rep throughout.

Leaving enough yarn to cast off, cont to end of third ball.

Cast off in rib.

TO FINISH

Weave in yarn ends.

Beaded Jewelry Purse

This cute jewelry purse is great for keeping valuables safe while making a great fashion statement. It is knitted in Rowan Denim yarn which is extremely practical, as it can be machine washed at relatively high temperatures.

The inspiration for this piece comes from the work of British designer Debbie Abrahams, and it is a great introduction to bead knitting and simple color changing.

Rowan Denim Yarn shrinks in length on the first washing and becomes denser and more colorfast. Washing is done once the piece is knitted, so don't be alarmed if the piece looks longer on the knitting needles than the finished piece.

Techniques Used

Casting On

Stockinette Stitch

Beading

Joining in a New Color

Knitting Two Stitches Together

Casting Off

MATERIALS

- 1 × 50 g ball of Rowan Denim in each of three colors Mid Blue (A), Pale Blue (B), and Cream (C)
- Pair size 6 (4 mm) needles
- 63 beads
- 1 button

MEASUREMENTS

5½ in. / 14 cm wide by 4¾ in. / 12 cm high

TENSION

20 sts and 28 rows to 4 in. / 10 cm square measured over st st using size 6 (4 mm) needles (before washing)

ABBREVIATIONS

B1 — yarn to front, slip next st, push bead up close to work, yarn to back.

See page 15.

NOTE

When working from a chart, odd-numbered rows are rs rows and are read from right to left, even-numbered rows are ws rows and are read from left to right.

BACK

With size 6 (4 mm) needles and C cast on 37 sts.

Cont in st st and stripe sequence of 2 rows C, work 3 rows B and 3 rows A until 44 rows are finished.

Shape Flap

Dec 1 st each end of every row until 7 sts rem.

Buttonhole row K2, k2tog, yf, k3.

Cont to dec 1 st each end of every row until 3 sts rem.

Cast off.

FRONT

Thread 63 beads onto yarn A.

With rs facing and yarn A, pick up and k37 sts along cast-on edge of back.

Starting with a p row, work 5 rows st st.

Starting with a k row, work 13 rows of chart, working a B1 where indicated.

Cont in st st until 43 rows have been worked in total. Cast off.

Edging

With size 6 (4 mm) needles and A, pick up and k34 sts along shaped edge. Cast off.

TO FINISH

Wash, following ball band instructions. Join side seams. Sew on button. Weave in yarn ends.

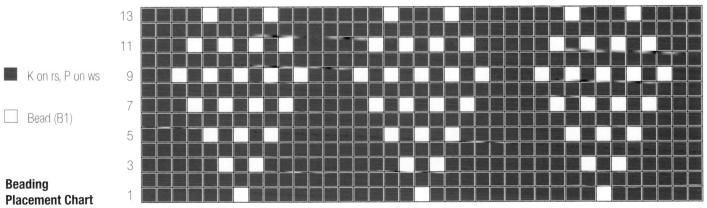

■ K on rs, P on ws

□ Bead (B1)

**Beading
Placement Chart**

Chunky Tasseled Belt

Belts are a real fashion-must and tend to be worn low and loose over the hips.

A belt like this is a fantastic project for new knitters, as it involves little, if no, shaping. Knitted in seed stitch, this belt has long tassels that hang from the buckle. These are made by casting stitches on and then off; thus this project is a great way of reinforcing the casting-on technique in your mind.

The yarn used for this project is a linen mix. Cotton and linen yarns are great for belts, since they tend not to stretch to the same extent as wool. A vast array of buckles are available from your local stores—choose a yarn color to match the buckle.

Techniques Used

Casting On

Knitting a Stitch

Purling a Stitch

Casting Off

MATERIALS

- 2 × 50 g hanks of Rowan Summer Tweed
- Pair each of size 11 (8 mm) and size 7 (4½ mm) needles
- 1 buckle

MEASUREMENTS

3¼ in. / 8 cm wide by 31½ in. / 80 cm long

TENSION

14 sts and 16 rows to 4 in. / 10 cm square over patt using size 11 (8 mm) needles and yarn double

ABBREVIATIONS

See page 15.

BELT

With size 11 (8 mm) needles and yarn used double; cast on 11 sts.

Row 1 K to end.

Row 2 K1tbl, * p1, k1tbl; rep from * to end.

Rep the last 2 rows until belt measures 31½ in. / 80 cm, ending with row 2.

Cast off.

Tassels (make 10)

With size 7 (4½ mm) needles, cast on 70 sts.

Cast off.

TO FINISH

Sew five tassels to each end of belt. Weave in yarn ends. Thread tassels through buckle when wearing.

Delicate Lacy Scarf

Fine yarns and lacy knitting can be quite a daunting prospect for a beginner knitter; however, this beautiful scarf is knitted using relatively large needles and a luxurious silk mohair-mix yarn that knits up quickly and can disguise uneven stitches.

The scarf is knitted in the most simple lace stitch on one row, with five knit rows following. These six rows are repeated throughout.

Techniques Used

Casting On
Knitting a Stitch
Slipping a Stitch
Making a Stitch
Knitting Two Stitches Together
Casting Off

MATERIALS

- 1 × 25 g ball of Rowan Kidsilk Haze
- Pair of size 7 (4½ mm) needles
- One size 9 (5½ mm) needle

MEASUREMENTS

Approx. 8¾ in. / 22 cm wide by 49 in. / 124 cm long

SCARF

With size 7 (4½ mm) needles, cast on 51 sts.

Row 1 K to end.

Row 2 K1, skpo, k to last st, m1, k1.

Rows 3 and 4 As row 1 and row 2.

Row 5 K to end.

Row 6 With size 9 (5½ mm) needles, k1, * yf, k2 tog; rep from * to end.

Rep the last 6 rows to end of ball, ending with row 5 and leaving enough yarn to cast off.

Cast off.

Projects *his knits*

Charcoal Raglan Sweater

This chunky man's sweater has raglan sleeves, which means that the top of the sleeve makes up part of the body. Raglans are very stylish and practical, and knitting one is an ideal way to learn about shaping. Depending upon how you decrease a stitch, i.e. whether you knit into the front or back of the stitches or slip a stitch over, your stitches will slant toward either the right or the left. Knitting a raglan will teach you to recognize which way your stitches lie and will help when you come to shape a more complicated design.

The neckline of this sweater features a small zipper which is sewn in once the knitting is finished.

Techniques Used

Casting On

Knitting a Stitch

Purling a Stitch

Double Rib

Stockinette Stitch

Casting Off

Slipping a Stitch

Knitting Two Stitches Together

Purling Two Stitches Together

Making a Stitch

MATERIALS

- 8 (9:10) × 100 g balls of Rowan Plaid
- Pair each of size 10½ (6½ mm) and size 11 (8 mm) needles
- 6 in. / 15 cm zipper

TENSION

11 sts and 15 rows to 4 in. / 10 cm square over st st using size 11 (8 mm) needles

ABBREVIATIONS

See page 15.

MEASUREMENTS

To fit chest		
34-36	38-40	42-44 in.
87-92	97-102	107-112 cm

Sweater Measurements

Chest		
43	45½	48 in.
109	116	122 cm

Length to shoulder		
24½	25¼	26 in.
62	64	66 cm

Sleeve length		
19¼	19¾	20 in.
49	50	51 cm

BACK

With size 10½ (6½ mm) needles, cast on 62 (66:70) sts.

Rib row 1 K2, * p2, k2; rep from * to end.

Rib row 2 P2, * k2, p2; rep from * to end.

Rep the last 2 rows 5 times more.

Change to size 11 (8 mm) needles.

Beg with a k row, cont in st st until back measures 15½ in. / 39 cm from cast on edge, ending with a p row.

Shape raglan armhole

Cast off 6 sts at beg of next 2 rows.

50 (54:58) sts.

Row 1 K2, skpo, k to last 4 sts, k2 tog, k2.

Row 2 P to end.

Rep the last 2 rows until 20 (22:24) sts rem, ending with row 1.

Next row P2 tog, p to last 2 sts, p2 tog tbl.

Leave these 18 (20:22) sts on a spare needle or holder.

FRONT

Work as given for back until 28 (30:32) sts rem.

Shape neck

Next row K2, skpo, k4, k2 tog, turn, and work on these sts for first side of neck.

Next row P to end.

Next row K2, skpo, k2, k2 tog.

Next row P to end.

Next row K2, skpo, k2 tog.

Next row P to end.

Next row K1, sl 1, k2 tog, psso.

Next row P2.

Leave these 2 sts on a holder.

With rs facing, slip center 8 (10:12) sts onto a holder, rejoin yarn to rem sts.

Next row Skpo, k4, k2 tog, k2.

Next row P to end.

Next row Skpo, k2, k2 tog, k2.

Next row P to end.

Next row Skpo, k2 tog, k2.

Next row P to end.

Next row K3 tog, k1.

Next row P2 tog and fasten off rem st.

SLEEVES

With size 10½ (6½ mm) needles cast on 34 (38:42) sts.

Work 12 rows rib as given for back on page 130.

Change to size 11 (8 mm) needles.

Starting with a k row, work 4 rows in st st.

Inc row K3, m1, k to last 3 sts, m1, k3.

Starting with a p row, work 5 rows in st st.

Rep the last 6 rows until there are 52 (56:60) sts.

Cont straight until sleeve measures 19¾ (20:20½) in. / 50 (51:52) cm from cast-on edge, ending with a p row.

Shape raglan top

Cast off 6 sts at beg of next 2 rows. 40 (44:48) sts

Next row K2, skpo, k to last 4 sts, k2 tog, k2.

Next row P to end.

Rep the last 2 rows until 10 (12:14) sts rem, ending with a k row.

Right sleeve only

Next row P2 tog, p to last 2 sts, p2 tog tbl.

Leave these 8 (10:12) sts on a stitch holder.

Left sleeve only

Next row P to last 2 sts, p2 tog tbl.

Leave these 9 (11:13) sts on a stitch holder.

NECKBAND

Join both back and right front raglan seams to their appropriate sleeves. Leave left-front raglan seam undone.

With size 10½ (6½ mm) needles and rs facing, k2 sts from holder, pick up and k7 sts down left front neck, k8 (10:12) sts from front neck holder, pick up and k8 sts up rs of front neck, k8 (10:12) sts from right sleeve, 18 (20:22) sts from back and 9 (11:13) sts from left sleeve. 60 (68:76) sts.

Row 1 (ws) P3, * k2, p2; rep from * to last 5 sts, k2, p3.

Row 2 K3, * p2, k2; rep from * to last 5 sts, p2, k3.

Rep the last 2 rows 5 times more and row 1 again.

Cast off in rib.

ZIPPER OPENING

Join left raglan seam leaving last 6 in. / 15 cm open.

With size 10½ (7 mm) needles and rs facing, pick up and k24 sts along each open edge. Cast off.

TO FINISH

Sew side and sleeve seams together. Sew in zipper using sewing thread. Weave in yarn ends.

Chunky V-Neck Sweater

Many women have knitted their sweetheart a sweater as a sign of their affection. Unfortunately, many projects undertaken at the first pang of true love tend to fall by the way side and are not completed.

This lovely, chunky sweater is a joy to knit, and because it is worked on large needles, it will not take too much of your time to complete.

If you do have to leave your knitting for a period of time, it is wise to undo the last row before you begin working again, because the needle can stretch the yarn and leave a ridge in the knitted fabric.

Techniques Used

Casting On

Knitting a Stitch

Stockinette Stitch

Casting Off

Knitting Two Stitches Together

Purling Two Stitches Together

Slipping a Stitch

Making a Stitch

MATERIALS

- 9 (10:11:12) × 100 g balls of Rowan Chunky
- Pair each of size 10½ (6½ mm) and size 11 (8 mm) needles

MEASUREMENTS

To fit chest

32-34	36-38	40-42	44-46 in.
82-86	92-97	102-107	112-117 cm

Sweater Measurements

Chest

38	42	46	50 in.
97	107	117	127 cm

Length to shoulder

26	26¾	27½	28½ in.
66	68	70	72 cm

Sleeve length

19¼	19¾	20	20½ in.
49	50	51	52 cm

TENSION

12 sts and 16 rows to 4 in. / 10 cm square over st st using size 11 (8 mm) needles

ABBREVIATIONS

See page 15.

BACK

With size 10½ (6½ mm) needles, cast on 60 (66:72:78) sts.

K 3 rows.

Change to size 11 (8 mm) needles.

Next row K to end.

Next row K3, p to last 3 sts, k3.

Rep the last 2 rows 3 times more.

Beg with a k row, cont in st st until back measures 16 (16½:17:17¼) in. / 41 (42:43:44) cm from cast-on edge, ending with a k row.

Change to size 10½ (6½ mm) needles.

K 3 rows.

Change to size 11 (8 mm) needles.

Shape armholes

Cast off 4 (5:6:7) sts at beg of next 2 rows. 52 (56:60:64) sts.

Cont in st st until back measures 26 (26¾:27½:28¼) in. / 66 (68:70:72) cm from cast-on edge, ending with a p row.

Shape shoulders

Cast off 16 (17:18:19) sts at beg of next 2 rows.

Cast off rem 20 (22:24:26) sts.

FRONT

Work as given for back until front measures 17¾ (18½:19:19¾) in. / 45 (47:48:50) cm from cast-on edge, ending with a p row.

Neck shaping

Next row K23 (25:28:29), k2tog, k1, turn and work on these sts for first side of neck.

Next row P to end.

Next row K to end.

Next row P1, p2tog, p to end.

Next row K to end.

Next row P to end.

Cont to dec in this way on every 3rd row until 16 (17:18:19) sts rem.

Work straight until front measures the same as back to shoulder, ending at armhole edge.

Shape shoulder

Cast off.

With rs facing, rejoin yarn to rem sts.

Next row K1, skpo, k to end.

Next row P to end.

Next row K to end.

Next row P to last 3 sts, p2tog tbl, p1.

Next row K to end.

Next row P to end.

Cont to dec in this way on every 3rd row until 16 (17:18:19) sts rem.

Work straight until front measures the same as back to shoulder, ending at armhole edge.

Cast off.

SLEEVES

With size 10½ (6½ mm) needles, cast on 40 (40:42:42) sts.

K 1 row.

Change to size 11 (8 mm) needles.

Starting with a k row, work 7 rows st st.

Change to size 10½ (6½ mm) needles.

K 3 rows.

Change to size 11 (8 mm) needles.

Starting with a k row, work 6 rows st st.

Inc row K3, m1, k to last 3 sts, m1, k3.

Starting with a p row, work 5 rows in st st.

Rep the last 6 rows until there are 60 (64:68:70) sts.

Cont straight until sleeve measures 19¼ (19¾:20:20½) in. / 49 (50:51:52) cm from cast-on edge, ending with a p row.

Mark each end of last row with a colored thread of yarn.

Work an additional 6 (6:8:8) rows.

Cast off.

NECKBAND

Join right shoulder seam.

With size 10½ (6½ mm) needles, pick up and k28 (28:29:29) sts down left side of front neck, 28 (28:29:29) sts up rs of front neck, 20 (22:24:26) sts from back neck. 76 (78:82:84) sts.

Next row K46 (48:51:53), skpo, k2tog, k26 (26:27:27).

Next row K25 (25:26:26), skpo, k2tog, k45 (47:50:52).

Next row K44 (46:49:51), skpo, k2tog, k24 (24:25:25).

Cast off, decreasing on this row, as before.

TO FINISH

Sew left shoulder and neckband seam together. Sew on sleeves, sewing last 6 (6:8:8) rows at top of sleeves into armhole shaping. Sew side and sleeve seams together. Weave in yarn ends.

Striped Casual Hat

This hat will provide great protection from the winter wind at a moment's notice, and can be slipped into a coat pocket in case the weather changes.

Knitted in a wool-and-cotton mix with a bold stripe detail, this hat will keep you warm while making a bold fashion statement.

This style of hat is often called a "beanie" and it can be knitted in any size, simply by adding or taking away a repeat of the pattern.

If you would like to make it longer, simply work a few rows before the first row of decreasing begins.

Techniques Used

Casting On

Knitting a Stitch

Purling a Stitch

Stockinette Stitch

Joining in a New Color

Slipping a Stitch

MATERIALS

- 2 × 50 g balls of Rowan Wool/Cotton DK in Navy
- 1 × 50 g ball each of Red and Green
- Pair of size 5 (3¾ mm) needles

MEASUREMENTS

To fit: Average man's head

TENSION

23 sts and 31 rows to 4 in. / 10 cm square over st st using size 5 (3¾ mm) needles

ABBREVIATIONS

See page 15.

HAT

With size 5 (3¾ mm) needles and Navy, cast on 134 sts.

Rib row 1 * K1, p1; rep from * to end.

Rep the last row 7 times more.

Starting with a k row, cont in st st as follows:

Work 8 rows Red and 8 rows Green.

Cont in Navy until hat measures 6 in. / 15 cm, ending with a p row.

Shape crown (decreasing)

Row 1 K1, [skpo, k10] 11 times, k1.

Row 2 P to end.

Row 3 K1, [skpo, k9] 11 times, k1.

Row 4 P to end.

Row 5 [K1, [skpo, k8] 11 times, k1.

Row 6 P to end.

Row 7 K1, [skpo, k7] 11 times, k1.

Row 8 P to end.

Row 9 K1, [skpo, k6] 11 times, k1.

Row 10 P to end.

Row 11 K1, [skpo, k5] 11 times, k1.

Row 12 P to end.

Row 13 K1, [skpo, k4] 11 times, k1.

Row 14 P to end.

Row 15 K1, [skpo, k3] 11 times, k1.

Row 16 P to end.

Row 17 K1, [skpo, k2] 11 times, k1.

Row 18 P to end.

Row 19 K1, [skpo, k1] 11 times, k1.

Row 20 P to end.

Next row K1, [skpo,] 11 times, k1.

Leaving a long end, cut off yarn and thread through rem sts. Pull up and secure.

TO FINISH

Sew seams together. Weave in yarn ends.

Chunky Scarf

This scarf is knitted with two strands of yarn at the same time, giving it a lovely texture and weight. It is perfect for those who want to practice with color changing, but don't want to embark on a complicated project. It is knitted in double rib, so it doesn't really have a right or wrong side, which makes it look great tied. The scarf can be tied in a variety of ways and, of course, can be knitted in any color combination—creating any number of looks, from stylish vintage to contemporary urban cool. A great gift.

Techniques Used

| Casting On |
| Knitting a Stitch |
| Purling a Stitch |
| Joining in a New Color |
| Casting Off |

MATERIALS

- 5 × 50 g balls of Rowan Wool/Cotton DK in Navy (M)
- 1 × ball mid Blue (C)
- Pair of size 10 (6 mm) needles

MEASUREMENTS

Approx. 9 in. / 23 cm by 56 in. / 142 cm

TENSION

18 sts and 20 rows to 4 in. / 10 cm square over rib patt, using size 10 (6 mm) needles and yarn double

ABBREVIATIONS

See page 15.

NOTE

Use yarn doubled throughout.

SCARF

With size 10 (6 mm) needles and M, cast on 42 sts.

Rib row 1 K2, * p2, k2; rep from * to end.

Rib row 2 P2, * k2, p2; rep from * to end.

Cont in rib and stripes of 10 rows M, [4 rows C, 8 rows M,] twice, 4 rows C.

Cont in M until scarf measures 47½ in. / 121 cm from cast-on edge.

Cont in stripes of [4 rows C, 8 rows M,] twice, 4 rows C, 12 rows M.

Cast off in rib.

TO FINISH

Weave in yarn ends.

Sleeveless V-Neck Vest

The ultimate in trendy urban chic! This sleeveless V-neck top is knitted in rice stitch in a Yorkshire tweed yarn, which gives it a wonderful varied color and texture. A rib is knitted on each edge, so the garment maintains a great shape.

The pattern is incredibly versatile—it can be paired with a shirt for a smarter look or a long-sleeved T-shirt, as shown, for a more casual approach.

Techniques Used

Casting On

Knitting a Stitch

Purling a Stitch

Casting Off

MATERIALS

■ 7 (7:8:8) × 50 g balls of Rowan Yorkshire Tweed DK

■ Pair of size 6 (4 mm) needles

TENSION

22 sts and 28 rows to 4 in. / 10 cm square over st st using size 6 (4 mm) needles

ABBREVIATIONS

See page 15.

MEASUREMENTS

To fit chest

34	36	38	40 in.
86	92	97	102 cm

V-neck Measurements

Chest

38	41	43½	46½ in.
97	104	111	118 cm

Length to shoulder

22½	23¼	24	24¾ in.
57	59	61	63 cm

BACK

With size 6 (4 mm) needles, cast on 109 (117:125:133) sts.

Row 1 P1, * k1 tbl, p1; rep from * to end.

Row 2 K1, * p1, k1; rep from * to end.

These 2 rows form the rib.

Work 6 more rows in rib.

Cont in patt, as follows:

Row 1 P1, * k1 tbl, p1; rep from * to end.

Row 2 K to end.

These 2 rows form the patt.

Cont until back measures 13¼ (13¾:14:14½) in. / 34 (35:36:37) cm from cast-on edge, ending with a k row.

Shape armholes

Cast off 7 (8:9:10) sts at beg of next 2 rows. 95 (101:107:113) sts.

Dec 1 st at each end of next and every foll alt row until 77 (81:85:89) sts rem.

Cont in patt until back measures 21¾ (22½:23¼:24) in. / 55 (57:59:61) cm from cast-on edge, ending with a k row.

Shape back neck and shoulders

Next row Patt 24 (25:26:27) sts, turn, and work on these sts for first side of neck.

Dec 1 st at neck edge on next 3 rows.

Next row Cast off 11 (11:12:12) sts, patt to end.

Work 1 row.

Cast off rem 10 (11:11:12) sts.

With rs facing, slip next 29 (31:33:35) sts on a holder, rejoin yarn to rem sts, patt to end.

Complete to match first side.

FRONT

With size 6 (4 mm) needles, cast on 109 (117:125:133) sts.

Row 1 (rs) K1 tbl, * p1, k1 tbl; rep from * to end.

Row 2 P1, * K1, p1; rep from * to end.

These 2 rows form the rib.

Work 6 more rows in rib.

Cont in patt, as follows:

Row 1 K1tbl, * p1, k1 tbl; rep from * to end.

Row 2 K to end.

These 2 rows form the patt.

Cont until front measures 13¼ (13¾:14:14½) in. / 34 (35:36:37) cm from cast-on edge, ending with a k row.

Shape armholes

Cast off 8 (9:10:11) sts at beg of next 2 rows. 93 (99:105:111) sts.

Front neck shaping

Next row Work 2 tog, patt 42 (45:48:51), work 2 tog, turn and work on these st for first side of neck.

Next row K to end.

Next row Work 2 tog, patt to last 2 sts, work 2 tog.

Rep the last 2 rows 7 (8:9:10) times.

Keeping armhole edge straight, cont to dec at neck edge on every alt row until 21 (22:23:24) sts rem.

Cont straight until work measures same as back to shoulder shaping, ending at armhole edge.

Shape shoulder

Next row Cast off 11 (11:12:12) sts, patt to end.

Work 1 row.

Cast off rem 10 (11:11:12) sts.

With rs facing, slip center st onto a holder, rejoin yarn to rem sts, patt to end.

Complete to match first side.

NECKBAND

Sew right shoulder seam.

With size 6 (4 mm) needles and rs facing, pick up and k57 (59:61:63) sts down left side of front neck shaping, k1 tbl from center front holder (mark this st), pick up and k56 (58:60:62) sts up rs of front neck, 6 (5:6:5) sts, down right side of back neck, patt across 29 (31:33:35) sts on back neck holder, pick up and k7 (6:7:6) sts up left side of back neck. 156 (160:168:172) sts.

Rib row 1 (ws) [P1, k1] 48 (49:52:53) times, p2 tog, p1, p2 tog tbl, [k1, p1] 27 (28:29:30) times, k1.

Rib row 2 [P1, k1 tbl] 27 (28:29:30) times, skpo, k1 tbl, k2 tog, [k1 tbl, p1] 47 (48:51:52) times, k1.

Work 4 more rows decreasing on these rows as set.

Cast off in rib, decreasing as before.

ARMBANDS

Join left shoulder and neckband seam.

With size 6 (4 mm) needles and rs facing, pick up and k107 (111:115:119) sts evenly round armhole edge.

Row 1 (ws) P1, * K1, p1; rep from * to end.

Row 2 K1 tbl, * p1, k1 tbl; rep from * to end.

Rep these 2 rows twice more. Cast off in rib.

TO FINISH

Sew side and armband seams together. Weave in yarn ends.

Cream Scarf

This small scarf takes just two balls of yarn to knit and is a great project for knitters wanting to master textured stitching.

Knitted in double seed stitch and using a fine mercerized cotton yarn, the scarf is ideal for any man wanting to add a finishing touch to an evening outfit, although there will doubtless be many ladies wanting to borrow it too!

The scarf looks great secured with a tie pin and would make a lovely gift.

Techniques Used

Casting On

Knitting a Stitch

Purling a Stitch

Casting Off

MATERIALS

■ 2 × 50 g balls of Rowan Cotton Glacé

■ Pair of size 3 (3¼ mm) needles

MEASUREMENTS

Approx. 5 in. / 13 cm by 39½ in. / 100 cm

TENSION

26 sts and 38 rows to 4 in. / 10 cm square over seed st, using size 3 (3¼ mm) needles

ABBREVIATIONS

See page 15..

SCARF

With size 3 (3¼ mm) needles cast on 34 sts.

Row 1 (RS) K2, * p2, k2; rep from * to end.

Row 2 P2, * k2, p2; rep from * to end.

Row 3 P2, * k2, p2; rep from * to end.

Row 4 K2, * p2, k2; rep from * to end.

These 4 rows form the patt and are rep throughout.

Cont in patt until scarf measures 39½ in. / 100 cm from cast-on edge, ending with a rs row.

Cast off in patt.

TO FINISH

Weave in yarn ends.

Men's Gloves

These gloves provide lots of practice with shaping techniques, so are not a project for a complete beginner. They are knitted in a wool cotton yarn, so it is easy to see each stitch and is simple to unravel if something goes wrong! Here they are shown in a practical, masculine color, but of course they can be knitted in an infinite number of yarn colors and textures. Perfect for keeping the hands toasty on a chilly day!

Techniques Used

Casting On

Knitting a Stitch

Purling a Stitch

Stockinette Stitch

Making a Stitch

Slipping a Stitch

MATERIALS

- 2 × 50 g balls of Rowan Wool/Cotton
- Pair each size 2 (2¾ mm) and size 5 (3¾ mm) needles

MEASUREMENTS

Gloves To fit medium hands

TENSION

23 sts and 31 rows to 4 in. / 10 cm square over st st using size 5 (3¾ mm) needles

ABBREVIATIONS

See page 15.

Right Glove

** With size 2 (3 mm) needles cast on 48 sts.

Rib row * K1, p1; rep from * to end.

Rep the last row 17 times more.

Change to size 5 (3¾ mm) needles.

Beg with a k row cont in st st.

Work 2 rows. **

Thumb shaping

Next row K25, m1, k1, m1, k22.

Work 3 rows.

Next row K25, m1, k3, m1, k22.

Work 3 rows.

Next row K25, m1, k5, m1, k22.

Work 3 rows.

Next row K25, m1, k7, m1, k22.

Cont to inc as set on every foll 4th row until there are 58 sts on needle.

Work 1 more row.

Divide for thumb

Next row K37, turn, cast on 3 sts.

Next row P16 sts.

Work 16 rows st st. Turn.

Next row K1, * skpo, k1; rep from * to end.

Next row P to end.

Next row K1, * skpo; rep from * to end.

Break yarn, thread through rem sts, draw up tightly, and join thumb seam.

With rs facing, pick up and k 3 sts from base of thumb, k to end. 48 sts.

Work 11 rows in st st.

*** First finger

Next row K30, turn, and cast on 2 sts.

Next row P15, turn, cast on 2 sts.

Work 20 rows st st.

Next row K1, * skpo, k1; rep from * to last st, k1.

Next row P to end.

Next row K1, * skpo; rep from * to last st, k1.

Break yarn, thread through rem sts, draw up tightly, and join first finger seam.

Second finger

With rs facing, pick up and k2 sts from base of first finger, k6, turn, cast on 2 sts.

Next row P15, turn, cast on 2 sts.

Work 22 rows st st.

Next row K1, * skpo, k1; rep from * to last st, k1.

Next row P to end.

Next row K1, * skpo; rep from * to last st, k1.

Break yarn, thread through rem sts, draw up tightly, and join second finger seam.

Third finger

With rs facing, pick up and k2 sts from base of second finger, k6, turn, cast on 2 sts.

Next row P15, turn, cast on 2 sts.

Work 20 rows st st.

Next row K1, * skpo, k1; rep from * to last st, k1.

Next row P to end.

Next row K1, * skpo; rep from * to last st, k1.

Break yarn, thread through rem sts, draw up tightly, and join third finger seam.

Fourth finger

With rs facing, pick up and k2 sts from base of third finger, k6, turn.

Next row P15.

Work 16 rows st st.

Next row K2, * skpo, k1; rep from * to last st, k1.

Next row P to end.

Next row K2, * skpo; rep from * to last st, k1.

Break yarn, thread through rem sts, draw up tightly, and join fourth finger seam.

Left Glove

Work as given for right glove from ** to **.

Thumb shaping

Next row K22, m1, k1, m1, k25.

Work 3 rows.

Next row K22, m1, k3, m1, k25.

Work 3 rows.

Next row K22, m1, k5, m1, k25.

Work 3 rows.

Next row K22, m1, k7, m1, k to end.

Cont to inc as set on every foll 4th row until there are 58 sts on needle.

Work 1 more row.

Divide for thumb

Next row K34, turn, cast on 3 sts.

Next row P16 sts.

Work 16 rows st st.

Next row K1, * skpo, k1; rep from * to end.

Next row P to end.

Next row K1, * skpo; rep from * to end.

Break yarn, thread through rem sts, draw up tightly and join thumb seam.

With rs facing, pick up and k3 sts from base of thumb, k to end. 48 sts.

Work 11 rows.

Complete as for right glove from *** to end.

TO FINISH

Weave in yarn ends.

Projects *home knits*

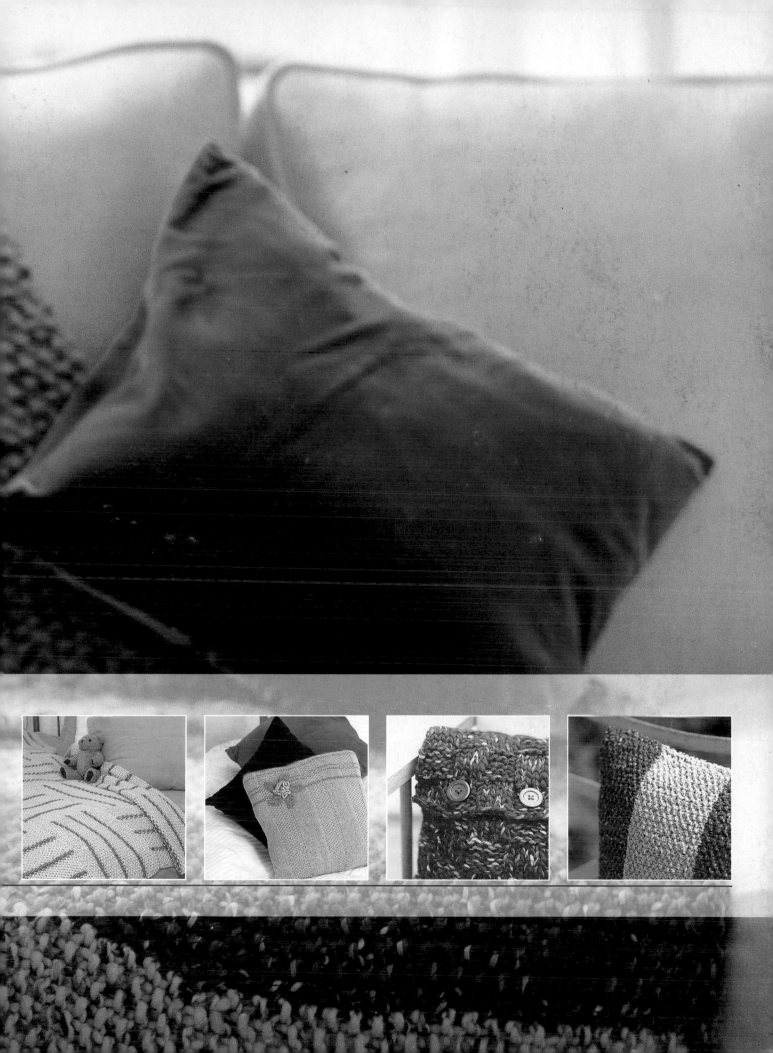

Flower-Detail Pillow Cover

This lovely pink pillow cover will look fantastic on a bed and it will add a touch of femininity to any room. The cover is worked in a clever, yet simple, stripe sequence and features differing textures and weights of yarn.

The flower detail is knitted separately then sewn in place. This would also make a great corsage that could be pinned to an outfit or worn as a brooch.

It is always a good idea to secure yarns at the beginning of the row when changing from one yarn to another, in order to avoid getting holes or loopy stitches in your knitting.

Techniques Used

Casting On

Knitting a Stitch

Purling a Stitch

Stockinette Stitch

Casting Off

Making a Stitch

Slipping a Stitch

Purling Two Stitches Together

MATERIALS

- 4 × 50 g balls of Rowan All Seasons Cotton in Pink (A)

- 1 × 50 g ball of Rowan Kid Classic in Pink (B)

- Pair each size 6 (4 mm) and size 8 (5 mm) knitting needles

- 7 buttons

- 16 in. / 41 cm square pillow form

MEASUREMENTS

Approx. 16 in. / 41 cm square

Seed-Stitch Afghan

This stylish and contemporary afghan will look perfect draped over a chair or sofa in a living room. The neutral tones give it a fresh, minimalist feel, and the textured seed stitch is fun to knit. This beautiful, chunky yarn is shot through with a length of ribbon in a complementary color and comes in a variety of shades. The afghan is knitted in four sections, which are then sewn together. The main section may be a little heavy to knit on straight needles, so for this, consider using a circular needle.

This is another good project for knitters wanting to master textured stitching. It can take quite a lot of practice to perfect an even tension, so be sure to sit comfortably and work in good light. Try to avoid putting your knitting down mid-row because this can cause the yarn to stretch.

Techniques Used

Casting On

Knitting a Stitch

Purling a Stitch

Seed Stitch

Casting Off

MATERIALS

- 10 × 100 g balls of Rowan Ribbon Twist in Cream
- 4 × 100 g balls Rowan Ribbon Twist in Gray
- Pair of size 17 (12 mm) needles

MEASUREMENTS

49 in. / 125 cm square

TENSION

7 sts and 12 rows to 4 in. / 10 cm square over seed st using size 17 (12 mm) needles

ABBREVIATIONS

See page 15.

AFGHAN

Main Section

With size 17 (12 mm) needles and Cream, cast on 46 sts.

Seed st row 1 * K1, p1; rep from * to end.

Seed st row 2 * P1, k1; rep from * to end.

These 2 rows form the seed st.

Cont in seed st until piece measures 49 in. / 125 cm from cast-on edge.

Cast off in seed st.

Side strips (make 2 gray and 2 cream)

With size 17 (12 mm) needles and Cream cast on 12 sts.

Seed st row 1 * K1, p1; rep from * to end.

Seed st row 2 * P1, k1; rep from * to end.

These 2 rows form the seed st.

Cont in seed st until piece measures 49 in. / 125 cm from cast-on edge.

Cast off in seed st.

TO FINISH

Sew side strips together, alternating colors, then sew strips to main piece. Weave in yarn ends.

Summer Deck Pillow

This bright pillow would look great in a hammock or among a pile of scattered pillows on the deck. It is knitted in soft, yet hard-wearing machine-washable cotton and is the perfect undertaking for knitters looking for their first Intarsia project.

Its geometric uniform design makes it an easy pattern to follow, with only a few color changes to each row, and the seed stitch gives the pillow a lovely texture.

It is a good idea to work out roughly how much yarn each colored square will take to knit and, allowing a little extra, use this to make up separate balls.

Techniques Used

Casting On

Knitting a Stitch

Purling a Stitch

Intarsia Color Work

Casting Off

MATERIALS

- 3 × 50 g hanks of Rowan Summer Tweed in each of Med Blue and Light Blue
- Pair of size 7 (4½ mm) needles
- Cushion pad 16 in. / 41 cm square

MEASUREMENTS

16 in. / 41 cm square

TENSION

18 sts and 24 rows to 4 in. / 10 cm square over seed st using size 7 (4½ mm) needles

ABBREVIATIONS

See page 15.

NOTE

To do Intarsia knitting, see page 50.

PILLOW

First side

With size 7 (4½ mm) needles and Light Blue, cast on 18 sts; using Medium Blue, cast on 18 sts; using Light Blue, cast on 18 sts; using Medium Blue, cast on 18 sts. 72 sts.

Row 1 * Using Medium Blue [k1, p1] 9 times, using Light Blue [k1, p1] 9 times; rep from * once more.

Row 2 * Using Light Blue [p1, k1] 9 times; using Medium Blue [p1, k1] 9 times; rep from * once more.

Rep the last 2 rows until piece measures 4 in. / 10 cm from cast-on edge, ending with a rs row.

Next row * Using Medium Blue p18; using Light Blue p18; rep from * once more.

Next row * Using Light Blue [k1, p1] 9 times; using Medium Blue [k1, p1] 9 times; rep from * once more.

Next row * Using Medium Blue [p1, k1] 9 times; using Light Blue [p1, k1] 9 times; rep from * once more.

Rep the last 2 rows until piece measures 8 in. / 20 cm from cast-on edge, ending with a rs row.

Next row * Using Light Blue p18; using Medium Blue p 18; rep from * once more.

* Using Medium Blue [k1, p1] 9 times; using Light Blue [k1, p1] 9 times; rep from * once more.

* Using Light Blue [p1, k1] 9 times; using Medium Blue [p1, k1] 9 times; rep from * once more.

Rep the last 2 rows until piece measures 12 in. / 30 cm from cast-on edge, ending with a rs row.

Next row * Using Medium Blue p18; using Light Blue p 18; rep from * once more.

Next row * Using Light Blue [k1, p1] 9 times; using Medium Blue [k1, p1] 9 times; rep from * once more.

Next row * Using Medium Blue [p1, k1]
9 times; using Light Blue [p1, k1]
9 times; rep from * once more.

Rep the last 2 rows until piece measures
16 in. / 40 cm from cast-on edge,
ending with a rs row.

Cast off.

Second side

With size 7 (4½ mm) needles and Light
Blue, cast on 72 sts.

Row 1 * K1, p1; rep from * to end.

Row 2 * P1, k1; rep from * to end.

Rep the last 2 rows until piece measures
4 in. / 10 cm from cast-on edge, ending
with a rs row.

Cut off Light Blue, join in Medium Blue.

Next row P to end.

Next row * K1, p1; rep from * to end.

Next row * P1, k1; rep from * to end.

Rep the last 2 rows until piece measures
8 in. / 20 cm from cast-on edge, ending
with a rs row.

Cut off Medium Blue, join in Light Blue.

Next row P to end.

Next row * K1, p1; rep from * to end.

Next row * P1, k1; rep from * to end.

Rep the last 2 rows until piece measures
12 in. / 30 cm from cast-on edge,
ending with a rs row.

Cut off Light Blue, join in Medium Blue.

Next row P to end.

Next row * K1, p1; rep from * to end.

Next row * P1, k1; rep from * to end.

Rep the last 2 rows until piece measures
16 in. / 40 cm from cast-on edge,
ending with a rs row.

Cast off.

TO FINISH

With right sides together, sew three
sides together. Turn to rs, insert pillow
form and join rem side. Weave
in yarn ends.

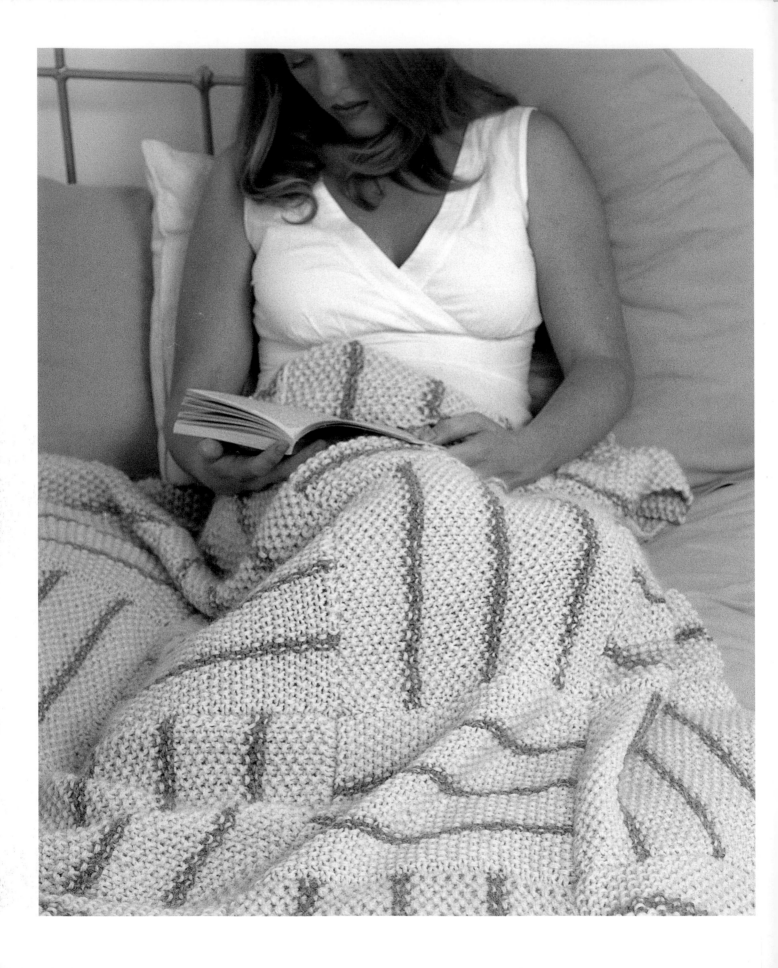

Patchwork Afghan

A large project such as a knitted afghan could be a very daunting prospect to a new knitter. This afghan, however, is knitted in squares that are then sewn together once complete. All squares are knitted with the same stripe sequence and pieced together to create a woven look.

The afghan can be made larger or smaller, depending on how many squares you choose to knit.

You could knit squares for this throw when you are on a train or bus, or watching television, and save more complicated projects for when you have more time to concentrate.

Techniques Used
Casting On
Knitting a Stitch
Purling a Stitch
Casting Off

MATERIALS

- 30 × 50 g balls Rowan Kid Classic in Cream
- 5 × balls Rowan Kid Classic in Lilac
- Pair of size 13 (9 mm) needles

MEASUREMENTS

60 in. / 150 cm wide × 71 in. / 180 cm long

TENSION

11 sts and 16 rows to 4 in. / 10 cm square over seed st using size 13 (9 mm) needles and yarn double

Each square measures 12 in. / 30 cm

ABBREVIATIONS

See page 15.

NOTE

Use yarn doubled throughout.

AFGHAN

Make 30 squares, as follows:

Leaving a long end for finishing, and using size 13 (9 mm) needles and Cream, cast on 35 sts.

Seed st row K1, * p1, k1; rep from * to end.

This row forms the seed st and is repeated throughout.

Work an additional 10 rows.

Work 2 rows in Lilac.

Work 12 rows in Cream.

Rep the last 14 rows once more and the first 13 of these 14 rows again.

Cast off in Seed st.

TO FINISH

Sew together the afghan as follows: 5 squares wide by 6 squares long, alternating direction of stripes between squares.

Index

Rowan Yarns Suppliers

United States

Purl
137 Sullivan Street,
New York 10012
tel: +1 212 420-8796
Web site: www.purlsoho.com

The Handworks Gallery
2911 Kavanaugh,
Little Rock, Arkansas 72205
tel: +1 501-664 6300
Web site:
www.handworksgallery.com

Jimmy Beans Wool
10065 Donner Pass Road,
Truckee, California 96161
tel: +1 530 582 9530
Web site: www.jimmybeanswool.com

Royal Yarns
404 Barnside Place,
Rockville, Maryland 20850
tel: +1 202 215 2300
Web site: www.royalyarns.com

Yarn Market
Ohio, USA. Web trader only.
tel: +1 888 996 9276
Web site: www.yarnmarket.com

Knitting.Garden
25 Longmeadow Road,
Uxbridge, Massachusetts 01569
tel: +1 888 381 9276
Web site: www.theknittinggarden.com

Sakonnet Purls
3988 Main Road,
Tiverton, Rhode Island 02878
tel: +1 888 624 9902
Web site: www.letsknit.com
E-mail: letsknit@letsknit.com

Colorful Stitches
48 Main Street, Lenox,
Massachusetts MA 01240
tel: +1 413 637 8206
Web site: www.colorful-stitches.com

Canada

Diamond Yarn
9697 Boulevard Street,
Laurent, Montreal, Canada
tel: +1 514 388 6188
Web site: www.diamondyarn.com
E-mail: diamond@diamondyarn.com

UK

Kangaroo
Merlins, Uckfield Road, Ingmer,
Lewes, East Sussex
tel: +44 (0)1273 814900
Web site: www.kangaroo.uk.com
E-mail: sales@kangaroo.uk.com

Shoreham Knitting
19 East Street, Shoreham By Sea,
West Sussex
tel: +44 (0)1273 461029
Web site: www.englishyarns.co.uk
E-mail: sales@englishyarns.co.uk

Up Country
Huddersfield Road,
Holmfirth, West Yorkshire
tel: +44 (0)1484 687803
Web site: www.upcountry.co.uk
E-mail: info@upcountry.co.uk

Colourway
Market Street, Whitland, Wales
tel: +44 (0)1994 241333
Web site: www.colourway.co.uk
E-mail: shop@colourway.co.uk

Get Knitted
Bristol. Web trader only.
tel: +44 (0)117 941 2600
Web site: www.getknitted.com

Laughing Hens
P.O. Box 176, St. Leonards-on-Sea,
East Sussex
tel: +44 (0)870 770 4352
Web site: www.laughinghens.com

Angel Yarns
Unit 1360, The Old Booker Building,
Chapel Road, Portslade,
East Sussex
tel: +44 (0)1273 411112
Web site: www.angelyarns.com
E-mail: tess@angelyarns.com

Buy Mail Ltd.
Bedfordshire. Web trader only.
Web site: www.buy-mail.com
E-mail: info@buy-mail.com

McAree Bros. Ltd.
55-59 King Street, Stirling, Scotland
tel: +44 (0)1786 465646
Web site: www.mcadirect.com

Stash
Godstall House, 4 Godstall Lane,
Chester, Cheshire
tel: +44 (0)1244 311136
Web site: www.celticove.com
E-mail: helen@celticove.com

France

Entrée des Fournisseurs
8 rue des Francs Bourgois, Paris
tel: +33 (0)1 48 87 58 98
Web site:
www.entreedesfournisseurs.com
E-mail: edf@club-internet.fr

Germany

Wolle & Design
Wolfshovener Strasse 76, Juelich
tel: +49 (0)2461/54735
Web site: www.wolleunddesign.de
E-mail: info@wolleunddesign.de

Italy

D L srl
Via Piave 24–26, Milan
tel: +39 39 02 339 101 80

Spain

Oyambre
Paul Claris 145, Barcelona
tel: +34 93 487 2672

Denmark

Tribsen
Web trader only.
Web site: www.tribsen.com

Sweden

Wincent
Norrtullsgatan 65, 113 45,
Stockholm
tel: +46 8 33 70 60
Web site: www.wincentgarner.se
E-mail: wincent@chello.se

Norway

Tjorven
Valkyriegt 17, Oslo
tel: +47 22 69 33 60
Web site: www.tjorven.no

Japan

Puppy Co Ltd
7-22-17 Nishigotanda
Shinagawaku, Tokyo
tel: +81 03 3494 2435
Web site: www.rowan-jaeger.com
E-mail: info@rowan-jaeger.com

Korea

My Knit Studio
(3F) 121 Kwan Hoon Dong, Seoul
tel: +82 822 722 0006
Web site: www.myknit.com
E-mail: myknit@myknit.com

Australia

Sunspun
185 Canterbury Road,
Melbourne, Victoria
tel: +61 (0)3 9830 1609
Web site: www.sunspun.com.au
E-mail: shop@sunspun.com.au

The Wool Shack
P.O. Box 228, Innaloo,
Perth, Western Australia
tel: +61 (0)8 9446 6344
Web site: www.thewoolshack.com
E-mail: info@thewoolshack.com

New Zealand

Alterknitives
P.O. Box 47, 961, Auckland
tel: +64 937 60337
E-mail: knitit@ihug.co.nz

South Africa

Arthur Bales Ltd.
62 4th Avenue, Linden,
Johannesburg
tel. +27 118 882 401
E-mail: arthurb@new.co.za

Author's Acknowledgments

With special thanks to Penny Hill, Project Co-ordinator, Pattern Checker, Knitter, and lifesaver! Thank you for your invaluable help and support!

Contributors/Designers:
Georgina Brant: Beaded Jewelry Purse p122;
Maureen Campbell Watts: Sky blue poncho and beret p100;
Amanda Crawford: Openwork shawl p65; Baby jacket and bootees p73;
Jane Crowfoot: Pastel beaded cardigan p107;
Penny Hill: Denim bonnet and bootees p62, Four-piece cashmere set p66, Seed stitch crib blanket p76, Baby beret and bootees p78, Rainbow poncho and hat p82, Ribbon-twist tasseled scarf p84, Chunky rainbow scarf set p89, Bobble hat p94, Vintage seed-stitch scarf p98, Sweater with beaded edging p104, Lacework fitted cap p111, Seed-stitch beret and scarf p113, Fitted turtleneck sweater p116, Woman's ribbed scarf p120, Chunky tasseled belt p124, Delicate lacy scarf p126, Charcoal raglan sweater p130, Chunky v-neck sweater p133, Striped casual hat p136, Chunky scarf p139, Sleeveless v-neck vest p140, Cream scarf p143, Men's gloves p144, Ribbon-twist pillow cover p150, Seed-stitch afghan p153, Summer deck pillow p154, Patchwork afghan p157;
Emma King: Flower-detail pillow cover p148, Striped rib hat and scarf p90, Striped glitter bag p92;
Julie Makin: Striped tote bag p102, Felted purse p114;
Helen McCarthy: Play pillow p70, Rainbow toy bag p86.